Outstanding Short Stories

Level 5

Selected and retold by G. C. Thornley
Series Editors: Andy Hopkins and Jocelyn Potter

Pearson Education Limited
Edinburgh Gate, Harlow,
Essex CM20 2JE, England
and Associated Companies throughout the world.

ISBN 0 582 41933 6

First published in the Longman Simplified English Series 1958
First published in the Longman Fiction Series 1993
This compilation first published 1996
Second impression 1997
This edition first published 1999

NEW EDITION

We are grateful to the following for permission to reproduce simplified versions of copyright
material: A. P. Watt Ltd. on behalf of the Royal Literary Fund for "Lord Mountdrago" by W. Somerset
Maugham from The Same Mixture As Before; the Literary Executors of the Estate of H. G. Wells for
"The Man Who Could Work Miracles" by H. G. Wells; the Trustees of the Wodehouse Estate for
"Lord Emsworth and the Girl Friend" from Blandings Castle by P. G. Wodehouse.

Typeset by Digital Type, London
Set in 11/14pt Bembo
Printed in Spain by Mateu Cromo, S. A. Pinto (Madrid)

Published by Pearson Education Limited in association with
Penguin Books Ltd, both companies being subsidiaries of Pearson Plc

For a complete list of the titles available in the Penguin Readers series please write to your local
Pearson Education office or to: Marketing Department, Penguin Longman Publishing,
5 Bentinck Street, London W1M 5RN.

Contents

Introduction

The stories in this collection were written in the nineteenth and early twentieth centuries by well-known writers from Britain, Ireland and the United States, and the collection presents the short story at its very best. A number of the writers represented here – Katherine Mansfield, Edgar Allan Poe, W. Somerset Maugham – are known above all for their short stories; others are more famous for their plays and novels. The stories are extremely varied in their subject matter. Some are about very ordinary people to whom something surprising happens, such as Fotheringay in 'The Man Who Could Work Miracles' by H. G. Wells, or Susan Bell in 'The Courtship of Susan Bell' by Anthony Trollope. Some contain unusual characters from the upper levels of society, like Lord Mountdrago in the Somerset Maugham story of the same name, or Oscar Wilde's 'model millionaire', Baron Hausberg. In 'Lord Emsworth and the Girl Friend', P. G. Wodehouse presents two very different characters from opposite ends of the social scale, between whom an unusual and moving relationship develops. Some of the stories are light-hearted and amusing; others are serious. Some have happy endings; others end in misery and death. What the stories have in common is that they are excellent examples of the short story – the central features of character and situation are expressed in a few well-chosen words that hold the reader's attention.

The English writer Herbert George Wells (1866–1946) is best remembered for his science fiction stories, but he also wrote about science, history and politics. His most famous books are *The Time Machine* (1895), *The Invisible Man* (1897) and *The War of the Worlds* (1898). His writings mirror the interest and excitement that was felt for science at the turn of the century. The combination of this feeling for the period and Wells's far-reaching imagination resulted in stories which make astonishing events seem quite believable.

Oscar Wilde (1854–1900) was an Irish writer of stories, plays and poetry. His mother, Lady Francesca Wilde, was a poet and society hostess. Wilde's childhood in Dublin was therefore quite unusual, and he met many of the leading figures of the day. He later studied at Oxford University, and began to write poetry and to develop his ideas on life and art. In 1905 he was sent to prison for what was then considered to be a sexual crime. When he was set free two years later, he wrote *The Ballad of Reading Gaol* (1898), the most powerful of his poems. He is best known now for a number of clever and amusing plays, particularly *Lady Windermere's Fan* (1892) and *The Importance of Being Ernest* (1895).

Pelham Grenville Wodehouse (1881–1975) was an English-born writer who later became an American citizen. For nearly the whole of his adult life he made a living by writing, producing nearly a hundred novels. He achieved international popularity with humorous stories about amusing characters in difficult situations. The best known of these characters are the helpless but likeable upper-class young man Bertie Wooster, and his manservant Jeeves, who helps him solve many of his problems. Wodehouse also wrote plays and musicals. In 1975 he received a title in recognition of his life's work.

Katherine Mansfield is the pen name of Kathleen Mansfield Beauchamp (1888–1923). Born in New Zealand, she went to London to study music and lived in Europe for most of her life. She had many unhappy love affairs, and in her later years she was struck by a lung disease that remained with her until she died. Some of her collections of short stories appeared after her death. She wrote sensitive, moving stories which often feature women and children as main characters.

Edgar Allan Poe (1809–49) led a short and unhappy life. He lost his parents at a young age and his wife after a short marriage, and his work was affected by his sufferings. Although he is known for horror and crime stories, the one chosen for this collection is a light-hearted account of a battle between two newspaper editors in small-town America.

The great English writer Anthony Trollope (1815–82) also had an unhappy start in life. His schooldays were made miserable by the fact that his father was frequently in debt and, as a result, the family was forced to move several times. When his father died, his mother supported the family through her writing. Anthony Trollope wrote about 60 works in all, mostly novels, but also some travel books and collections of short stories. He is most famous for two important series of books: the Barchester series, which is based around the lives of church officials and their families in the fictional area of Barsetshire, and the Palliser series, set in the world of politics and government.

William Somerset Maugham (1874–1965) was born in Paris to an Irish family. His mother died when he was eight. After his father's death two years later, he was sent to England to live with an uncle. Maugham studied medicine in Germany and England before deciding to become a writer. During the First World War he served as an intelligence officer and developed a love of travelling that stayed with him for the rest of his life. His ability to involve the reader very quickly made him an excellent short story writer, and he produced a number of collections. His most famous novel is *Of Human Bondage* (1915).

The Man Who Could Work Miracles   *H. G. Wells*

Until he was thirty years old, Fotheringay did not believe in miracles. In fact he discovered his own unusual powers at the moment when he was claiming that miracles were quite impossible. He was having a drink at his local inn, and Toddy Beamish was driving him to the limits of his patience by disagreeing with everything he said.

'So *you* say,' answered Beamish whenever Fotheringay spoke.

There were present, besides these two, a very dusty cyclist; the innkeeper, Cox; and fat Miss Maybridge, who served behind the bar. She was standing with her back to Mr Fotheringay, washing glasses; the others were watching him.

'Listen, Mr Beamish,' said Mr Fotheringay, annoyed by his opposition. 'Let us clearly understand what a miracle is. It's something against the laws of nature done by the power of Will, something that couldn't happen without being specially willed.'

'So *you* say,' said Mr Beamish.

The cyclist agreed with Mr Fotheringay, but the innkeeper did not express an opinion.

'For example,' said Mr Fotheringay, 'here would be a miracle. That lamp, in the normal course of nature, couldn't burn like that upside down, could it, Beamish?'

'*You* say it couldn't,' said Beamish.

'And you?' said Fotheringay. 'You don't mean to say – ?'

'No,' said Beamish at last. 'No, it couldn't.'

'Very well,' said Mr Fotheringay. 'Then here comes someone, perhaps myself, and stands here, perhaps, and says to that lamp, as I might do, collecting all my will – "Turn upside down without breaking, and go on burning steadily," and – Hullo!'

It was enough to make anyone say 'Hullo!' The impossible had happened. The lamp hung upside down in the air, burning quietly with its flame pointing down. It was as solid as ever a lamp was.

Mr Fotheringay stood with a finger stretched out and the troubled face of one expecting a terrible crash. The cyclist, who was sitting next to the lamp, jumped away. Miss Maybridge turned and cried out. For nearly three seconds the lamp remained as it was. A faint cry of pain came from Mr Fotheringay. 'I can't keep it up,' he said, 'any longer.' The lamp suddenly fell, broke on the floor, and went out.

It was lucky that it had a metal container, or the whole place would have been on fire. Mr Cox was the first to speak, remarking that Mr Fotheringay was a fool. Fotheringay himself was astonished at what had happened. The conversation which followed gave no explanation of the matter, and the general opinion agreed with Mr Cox's view that Fotheringay was a fool for playing such a trick. His own mind was terribly confused, and he rather agreed with them.

He went home red-faced and hot. He watched each of the ten street lamps nervously as he passed it. It was only when he found himself in his bedroom that he was able to think clearly.

He had taken off his shoes and was sitting on the bed, saying for the seventeenth time, 'I didn't want the thing to turn over,' when he remembered that just by saying the commanding words, he had willed the thing to happen. He decided to try his new powers again.

He pointed to the candle and collected his thoughts together, though he felt that he was behaving foolishly. But in a second that feeling disappeared. 'Be raised up,' he said. The candle rose up, hung in the air for a moment, and then fell with a crash on his table, leaving him in darkness.

For a time Mr Fotheringay sat there, perfectly still. 'It did happen,' he said. 'And how I'm going to explain it, I don't know.'

He felt in his pockets for a match. He could find none, so he felt on the table. He tried his coat, and there were none there, and then it came to his mind that miracles were possible even with matches. He stretched out a hand. 'Let there be a match in that hand,' he said. He felt a light object fall across his hand, and his fingers closed on a match.

After several useless attempts to light this, he threw it down; and then he realized that he could have willed it to be lit. He did so, and saw it burning on the table. He picked it up quickly, and it went out. He became more adventurous and put the candle back in its place. 'Be lit!' said Mr Fotheringay, and immediately the candle burst into flame. For a time he looked at it and then he looked carefully into the mirror.

'What about miracles now?' said Mr Fotheringay, speaking to his own shadowed face.

Mr Fotheringay was becoming very confused. So far as he could understand, he had only to will things and they would happen. After his first experiences, he wished to be more careful. But he lifted a sheet of paper into the air, and turned a glass of water pink and then green, and got himself a new toothbrush. By the early hours of the morning he had decided that willpower must be unusual and strong. The fears of his first discovery were now mixed with pride and thoughts of how he could use his powers to his advantage. He heard the church clock strike one, and undressed in order to get into bed without further delay. As he struggled to undress, he had a wonderful idea. 'Let me be in bed,' he said, and found himself there. 'Undressed,' he said and, finding the sheets cold, added quickly, 'and in a soft woollen nightshirt. Ah!' he said with pleasure. 'And now let me be comfortably asleep . . .'

He awoke at his usual hour, and wondered if his experiences had been a dream. He decided to test his skills again. He had three eggs for breakfast; two were supplied by his housekeeper; one was a much better egg, laid, cooked and served by his own unusual will. He hurried off to work very excited. All day he could do no work because of his astonishing new self-knowledge, but this did not matter because he did all the work by a miracle in the last ten minutes.

As the day passed, his state of mind changed from wonder to pleasure. It was clear that he must be careful how he lifted anything that was breakable, but in other ways his powers seemed more exciting the more he thought about them. He increased his personal property by making new things for himself, but he could see that he must be careful about that too. People might wonder how he got them.

After supper he went out for a walk on a quiet street to try a few miracles in private by the gas works.

His attempts could perhaps have been more interesting, but apart from his willpower Mr Fotheringay was not a very interesting man. He stuck his walking stick into the ground and commanded the dry wood to grow flowers. The air was immediately full of the smell of roses, but his satisfaction ended when he heard footsteps. He was afraid that someone would discover his powers, and he said quickly to the stick, 'Go back.' What he meant was, 'Change back', but the stick went backwards at high speed, and there came a shout of anger.

'Who are you throwing rose bushes at, you fool?' cried a voice.

'I'm sorry,' said Fotheringay. He saw Winch, one of the three local policemen, coming towards him.

'What do you mean by it?' asked the policeman. 'Hullo! It's you, is it? The man who broke the lamp at the inn!'

'I don't mean anything by it,' Said Mr Fotheringay. 'Nothing at all.'

'Why did you do it, then? Do you know that stick hurt?'

For the moment Fotheringay could not think why he had done it. His silence seemed to anger Mr Winch. 'You've been attacking the police, young man, this time. That's what *you've* done.'

'Listen, Mr Winch,' said Mr Fotheringay, angry and confused. 'I'm very sorry. The fact is . . .'

'Well?'

He could think of no answer except the truth. 'I was working a miracle.'

'Working a . . .! Listen! Don't talk nonsense. Working a miracle! Really! Miracle! Well, that's very funny! You're the man who doesn't believe in miracles . . . The fact is, this is another of your foolish tricks. Now I tell you – '

But Mr Fotheringay never heard what Mr Winch was going to tell him. He realized that he had given his valuable secret to the whole world. He became violently angry and shouted, 'Listen, I've had enough of this. I'll show you a foolish trick. Disappear! Go now!'

He was alone.

Mr Fotheringay performed no more miracles that night, and he did not trouble to see what had happened to his flowering stick. He returned to the town, afraid and very quiet, and went to his bedroom. 'Good heavens!' he said. 'It's a powerful gift – an extremely powerful gift. I didn't mean to go that far. I wonder where Winch has gone.'

He sat on the bed and took off his shoes. He had a happy thought and sent the policeman to San Francisco, and went to bed. In the night he dreamt of Winch's anger.

The next day Fotheringay heard two interesting pieces of news. Someone had planted a most beautiful climbing rose near Mr Gomshott's house, and everyone was looking for Policeman Winch.

Mr Fotheringay was thoughtful all that day, and performed no miracles except some to help Winch, and the miracle of completing his day's work on time. Most of the time he was thinking of Winch.

On Sunday evening he went to church, and strangely enough the minister, Mr Maydig, spoke about 'things that are not lawful'.

Mr Fotheringay was not a regular churchgoer but decided to tell Mr Maydig about his powers, and to ask his advice.

Mr Maydig, a thin, excitable man with a long neck, was pleased when the young man asked to speak to him. He took him to his study, gave him a comfortable seat and, standing in front of a cheerful fire, asked Mr Fotheringay to state his business.

At first Mr Fotheringay found some difficulty in opening the subject. 'You will hardly believe me, Mr Maydig ...' and so on for some time. He tried a question at last, and asked Mr Maydig his opinion of miracles.

'You don't believe, I suppose,' said Fotheringay, 'that some common sort of person – like myself, for example – might have something strange inside him that made him able to do things by willpower?'

'It's possible,' said Mr Maydig. 'Something of that sort, perhaps, is possible.'

'If I may try with something here, I think I can show you what I mean,' said Mr Fotheringay. 'Now that pot on the table, for example. I want to know whether this is a miracle or not.'

He pointed to the pot and said, 'Be a bowl of flowers.'

The pot did as it was ordered.

Mr Maydig jumped violently at the change, and stood looking from Fotheringay to the flowers. He said nothing. Slowly he leaned over the table and smelt the flowers; they were fresh and very fine. Then he looked at Fotheringay again.

'How did you do that?' he asked.

Mr Fotheringay said, 'I just told it – and there you are. Is that a miracle, or what is it? And what do you think is the matter with me? That's what I want to ask.'

'It's a most astonishing thing.'

'And last week I didn't know I could do things like that. It came quite suddenly. It's something strange about my will, I suppose.'

'Is that − the only thing? Could you do other things besides that?'

'Oh, yes!' said Mr Fotheringay. 'Anything.' He thought a little. 'Look!' He pointed. 'Change into a bowl of fish. You see that, Mr Maydig?'

'It's unbelievable. You are either a most unusual . . . But no . . .'

'I could change it into anything,' said Mr Fotheringay. 'Be a bird, will you?'

In another moment a blue bird was flying round the room and Mr Maydig had to bend his head every time it came near him. 'Stop there, will you?' said Mr Fotheringay; and the bird hung still in the air. 'I could change it back to a bowl of flowers,' he said, and after placing the bird on the table he worked that miracle. 'I expect you want your pot back,' he said, and brought back the pot.

Mr Maydig said nothing while he watched all these changes, but he gave a small cry every now and then. He picked up the pot carefully, examined it, and put it back on the table. 'Well!' was the only expression of his feelings.

'Now after that, it's easier to explain what I wanted to ask you,' said Mr Fotheringay; and he told the whole story to Mr Maydig, beginning with the lamp at the inn and several times mentioning Winch. Mr Maydig listened carefully, and interrupted when Fotheringay was talking about the third egg he had caused to appear at breakfast.

'It's possible,' said Maydig, 'but astonishing. The power to work miracles is a gift and a very rare gift. Yes − yes. Go on. Go on.'

Mr Fotheringay went on to talk about Winch. 'It's this that troubles me most,' he said, 'and I'm in need of advice mostly about Winch. Of course he's in San Francisco − wherever San Francisco may be − but it's awkward for both of us, Mr Maydig. I don't see how he can understand what has happened, and he must be very angry with me. He may be trying to come back here to get me. I send him back by a miracle every few hours, when I think of it. Of course he won't be able to understand that, and if he buys a ticket every time it will cost him a lot of money. I've done the best I could for him. But I'm in a very difficult position.'

Mr Maydig looked serious. 'Yes, you are. How are you going to end it?' He became confused. 'But we'll leave Winch for a little and discuss the whole subject,' continued Mr Maydig. 'I don't think this is criminal at all. No, it's just miracles, miracles of the very highest class.'

He began to walk around. Mr Fotheringay sat with his arm on the table and his head on his arm, looking worried. 'I don't see what I can do about Winch,' he said.

'If you can work miracles,' said Mr Maydig, 'you can solve the problem of Winch. My dear sir, you are a most important man – a man of the most astonishing possibilities. The things you could do . . .'

'Yes, I've thought of a thing or two,' said Mr Fotheringay. 'But I thought it better to ask someone.'

'Quite right,' said Mr Maydig. He stopped and looked at Fotheringay. 'It's almost an unlimited gift. Let us test your powers.'

And so, though it is hard to believe, in the little study on the evening of Sunday, 10 November, 1896, Mr Fotheringay, urged on by Mr Maydig, began to work miracles. The reader's attention is specially called to the date. He will object – probably he has already objected – that certain events in this story are improbable; that if these things had really happened they would have been in the newspapers long ago. The details which follow now will be particularly hard to accept, because they show, among other things, that he or she, the reader, must have been killed in a strange and violent manner in the past. As a matter of fact the reader *was* killed. In the remaining part of this story that will become perfectly clear, and every reasonable reader will accept the fact.

8

At first the miracles worked by Mr Fotheringay were little things with cups and such things. After he and Mr Maydig had worked several of these, their sense of power grew, their imagination increased, and they wanted to do greater things. Their first larger miracle was connected with the meal to which Mr Maydig led Mr Fotheringay. It was not a good meal, and Mr Maydig was expressing his sorrow at this when Mr Fotheringay saw his opportunity.

'Don't you think, Mr Maydig,' he said, 'I might . . .?'

'My dear Fotheringay! Of course! I didn't think.'

Mr Fotheringay waved his hand. 'What shall we have?' he said, and following Mr Maydig's orders produced a much better meal.

They sat for a long time at their supper, talking as equals. 'By the way,' said Mr Fotheringay, 'I might be able to help you with *all* your meals.' He put some food into his mouth. 'I was thinking that I might be able to work a miracle on your housekeeper, Mrs Minchin.'

Mr Maydig put down his glass and looked doubtful. 'She strongly objects to being troubled, you know, Mr Fotheringay. And – as a matter of fact – it's after 11 o'clock, and she's probably in bed and asleep.'

Mr Fotheringay considered these objections. 'I don't see why it shouldn't be done in her sleep.'

For a time Mr Maydig opposed the idea, and then he agreed. Mr Fotheringay gave his orders, and the two gentlemen went on with their meal, feeling slightly anxious. While they were talking of Mrs Minchin, they heard some strange noises coming from upstairs. Mr Maydig left the room quickly. Mr Fotheringay heard him calling the housekeeper and then his footsteps going softly up to her.

In a minute or two Mr Maydig returned, his face smiling. 'Wonderful!' he said. 'Wonderful!'

He began walking around the room. 'Poor woman! A most

impressive change! She had got up out of her sleep to get rid of a bottle of alcohol that she was keeping in her room. And she admitted it too, through the crack of the door. This may be the start of the most wonderful possibilities. If we can make this change in *her* . . .'

'And about Mr Winch . . .' said Fotheringay.

Mr Maydig waved the Winch difficulty away, and made some proposals. These proposals are not part of this story, but they were good-natured and quite astonishing. In the early hours Mr Maydig and Mr Fotheringay were outside under the moon, Mr Maydig waving his arms, Mr Fotheringay no longer afraid of his greatness. They changed all heavy drinkers into good men; they changed all alcohol into water. They improved the running of the trains and the soil of One Tree Hill, and they were considering what could be done with the broken part of South Bridge. 'The place,' said Mr Maydig, 'won't be the same place tomorrow. How surprised and thankful everyone will be!' And just at that moment the church clock struck three.

'Oh!' said Mr Fotheringay, 'that's three o'clock! I must be going home. I've got to be at work by eight o'clock.'

'We're only just starting,' said Mr Maydig, full of the sweetness of unlimited power. 'We're only beginning. Think of all the good we're doing. When people wake . . .'

'But . . .' said Mr Fotheringay.

Mr Maydig seized his arm. His eyes were bright and wild.

'My dear man,' he said, 'there's no hurry. Look!' He pointed to the moon. 'Stop it!' he said. 'Why not?'

Mr Fotheringay looked at the full moon.

'That's too much,' he said.

'Why not?' said Mr Maydig. 'Of course the moon doesn't stop. You stop the turning of the earth, you know. Time stops. It isn't wrong.'

'H'm!' said Mr Fotheringay. 'Well, I'll try.'

He spoke to the earth. 'Just stop turning, will you?' said Mr Fotheringay.

Immediately he was flying head over heels through the air at high speed. Although he was turning round and round, he was able to think. He thought in a second, and willed, 'Let me come down safe and unhurt.'

He willed it only just in time, for his clothes, heated by his rapid movement through the air, were beginning to burn. He came down on some freshly turned earth. A large amount of stone, very like the clock tower which had stood in the middle of the market square, hit the earth near him and broke into pieces. A flying cow hit one of the larger blocks and burst like an egg. There was a crash that made all the most violent crashes of his life sound like falling dust. A great wind roared all round him, so that he could hardly lift his head to look. For a time he was too breathless even to see where he was or what had happened.

'Good heavens!' he said. 'I was nearly killed! What has gone wrong? Storms and thunder! And only a minute ago, a fine night. *What* a wind! It's Maydig's fault. If I go on like this, I'm going to have a terrible accident . . . Where's Maydig?'

He looked around him as well as he could. The appearance of things was extremely strange. 'The sky's all right,' said Mr Fotheringay. 'And that's about all that is right. There's the moon overhead. Just as it was. Bright as midday. But the rest? Where's the village? Where's anything? And what started this wind? I didn't order a wind.'

Mr Fotheringay struggled unsuccessfully to get to his feet, and remained on the ground.

Far and wide nothing could be seen through the dust that flew in the wind except piles of earth and ruins. No trees, no houses, no familiar shapes, only disorder and a rapidly rising storm.

You see, when Mr Fotheringay stopped the earth, he said nothing about the things on its surface. And the earth turns so

11

fast that parts of its surface are travelling at rather more than a thousand miles an hour; in England, at more than half that speed. So the village, and Mr Maydig, and Mr Fotheringay, and everything and everybody had been thrown violently forward at about nine miles per second – that is to say, much more violently than if they had been fired out of a gun. And every human being, every living creature, every house and every tree – all the world as we know it – had been completely destroyed. That was all.

These things Mr Fotheringay did not fully understand. But he saw that his miracle had gone wrong, and with that a great hatred of miracles came on him. He was in darkness now, for the clouds had covered over the moon. A great roaring of wind and water filled the earth and sky, and he saw a wall of water pouring towards him.

'Maydig!' cried Mr Fotheringay's weak voice in the roar of the storm. 'Here! – Maydig!'

'Stop!' cried Mr Fotheringay to the wall of water. 'Oh, stop!'

'Just a moment,' said Mr Fotheringay to the storm and the thunder. 'Stop just a moment while I collect my thoughts . . . And now what *shall* I do?' he said. 'Oh, I wish Maydig was here.'

'I know,' said Mr Fotheringay. 'And let's have it right *this* time. Let nothing that I'm going to order happen until I say "Off" . . . Oh, I wish I had thought of that before!'

He lifted his little voice against the roaring wind, shouting louder and louder in an attempt to hear himself speak. 'Now! Remember what I said just now. In the first place, when all I've asked for is done, let me lose my power to work miracles; let my will become just like anybody else's will, and let all these dangerous miracles be stopped. That's the first thing. And the second is – let everything be just as it was before that lamp turned upside down. Do you understand? No more miracles, everything as it was – me back at the inn just before I had my drink. That's it! Yes.'

12

He dug his fingers into the earth, closed his eyes, and said 'Off!'

Everything became perfectly still. He knew that he was standing up.

'So *you* say,' said a voice.

He opened his eyes. He was at the inn, arguing about miracles with Toddy Beamish. He had a feeling of some great thing forgotten, which passed immediately. You see, except for the loss of his powers, everything was back as it had been; his mind and memory were now just as they had been at the time when this story began. So he knew nothing of all that is told here, knows nothing of all that is told here to this day. And among other things, of course, he still did not believe in miracles.

'I tell you that miracles can't possibly happen,' he said, 'and I'm prepared to prove it.'

'That's what *you* think,' said Beamish. 'Prove it if you can.'

'Listen, Mr Beamish,' said Mr Fotheringay. 'Let us clearly understand what a miracle is . . .'

The Model Millionaire   *Oscar Wilde*

Unless one is wealthy there is no use in being a charming person. The poor should be ordinary and practical. It is better to have a permanent income than to be interesting. These are the great truths of modern life which Hughie Erskine never realized. Poor Hughie! He was not, we must admit, a man of great intelligence. He never said a clever or even an unkind thing in his life. But then he was wonderfully good-looking, with his brown hair, his clear-cut features, and his grey eyes. He was as popular with men as he was with women, and he had every quality except that of making money. His father, on his death, had left him his sword and a *History of the Peninsular War* in 15 parts. Hughie hung the first above his mirror, put the second on a shelf, and lived on two hundred pounds a year that an old aunt allowed him. He had tried everything. He had bought and sold shares for six months; but how could he succeed among experienced men? He had been a tea trader for a little longer, but he had soon tired of that. Then he had tried selling wine, but nobody bought any. At last he became nothing, a charming, useless young man with perfect features and no profession.

To make matters worse, he was in love. The girl he loved was Laura Merton, the daughter of a former army officer who had lost his temper and his health in India, and had never found either of them again. Hughie loved her so much that he was ready to kiss her feet; and Laura loved him too. They were the best-looking pair in London, and had no money at all. Her father was very fond of Hughie, but would not hear of any marriage plans.

'Come to me, my boy, when you have got ten thousand pounds of your own, and we will see about it,' he used to say.

One morning, Hughie called in to see a great friend of his,

Alan Trevor. Trevor was a painter. Of course, few people are not these days. But he was also an artist, and artists are rather rare. He was a strange, rough man, with a spotty face and an overgrown red beard. But when he took up the brush he was a real master, and his pictures were very popular. He had been much attracted by Hughie at first, it must be admitted, just because of his personal charm. 'The only people a painter should know,' he used to say, 'are people who are both beautiful and stupid, people who are a pleasure to look at and restful to talk to.' But after he got to know Hughie better, he liked him quite as much for his bright, cheerful spirits, and his generous, carefree nature, and had asked him to visit whenever he liked.

When Hughie came in, he found Trevor putting the finishing touches to a wonderful life-size picture of a beggar. The beggar himself was standing on a raised platform in a corner of the room. He was a tired old man with a lined face and a sad expression. Over his shoulder was thrown a rough brown coat, all torn and full of holes; his thick boots were old and mended, and with one hand he leant on a rough stick, while with the other he held out his old hat for money.

'What an astonishing model!' whispered Hughie, as he shook hands with his friend.

'An astonishing model?' shouted Trevor at the top of his voice; 'I should think so! Such beggars are not met with every day. Good heavens! What a picture Rembrandt would have made of him!'

'Poor old man!' said Hughie. 'How miserable he looks! But I suppose, to you painters, his face is his fortune.'

'Certainly,' replied Trevor, 'you don't want a beggar to look happy, do you?'

'How much does a model get for being painted?' asked Hughie, as he found himself a comfortable seat.

'A shilling an hour.'

'And how much do you get for your picture, Alan?'

'Oh, for this I get two thousand pounds.'

'Well, I think the model should have a share,' cried Hughie, laughing; 'he works quite as hard as you do.'

'Nonsense, nonsense! Look at the trouble of laying on the paint, and standing all day in front of the picture! It's easy, Hughie, for you to talk. But you mustn't talk; I'm busy. Smoke a cigarette, and keep quiet.'

After some time the servant came in, and told Trevor that the frame maker wanted to speak to him.

'Don't run away, Hughie,' he said, as he went out, 'I will be back in a moment.'

The old beggar took advantage of Trevor's absence to rest for a moment. He looked so miserable that Hughie pitied him, and felt in his pockets to see what money he had. All he could find was a pound and some pennies. 'Poor old man,' he thought, 'he needs it more than I do, but I shan't have much money myself for a week or two'; and he walked across the room and slipped the pound into the beggar's hand.

The old man jumped, and a faint smile passed across his old lips. 'Thank you, sir,' he said, 'thank you.'

Then Trevor arrived, and Hughie left, a little red in the face at what he had done. He spent the day with Laura, who was charmingly cross that he had given away a pound, and had to walk home because he had no money for transport.

That night he went to his club at about 11 o'clock, and found Trevor sitting by himself in the smoking room.

'Well, Alan, did you finish the picture all right?' he asked.

'Finished and framed, my boy!' answered Trevor; 'and, by the way, that old model you saw has become very fond of you. I had to tell him all about you – who you are, where you live, what your income is, what hopes you have . . .'

'My dear Alan,' cried Hughie, 'I shall probably find him

16

waiting for me when I go home. But, of course, you are only joking. Poor old man! I wish I could do something for him. I think it is terrible that anyone should be so miserable. I have got piles of old clothes at home – do you think he would like any of them? His clothes were falling to bits.'

'But he looks wonderful in them,' said Trevor. 'I would never want to paint him in good clothes. But I'll tell him of your offer.'

'Alan,' said Hughie seriously, 'you painters are heartless men.'

'An artist's heart is in his head,' replied Trevor; 'and besides, our business is to show the world as we see it, not to make it better. And now tell me how Laura is. The old model was quite interested in her.'

'You don't mean to say you talked to him about her?' said Hughie.

'Certainly I did. He knows all about the cruel father, the lovely Laura, and the ten thousand pounds.'

'You told the old beggar all about my private affairs?' cried Hughie.

'My dear boy,' said Trevor, smiling, 'that old beggar, as you call him, is one of the richest men in Europe. He could buy all London tomorrow and still have money in the bank. He has a house in every capital, eats off plates of gold, and can prevent Russia going to war when he wishes.'

'What on earth do you mean?' cried Hughie.

'What I say,' said Trevor. 'The old man you saw today in my room was Baron Hausberg. He is a great friend of mine, buys all my pictures and that sort of thing, and asked me a month ago to paint him as a beggar. There's nothing surprising about that. These rich men have some strange ideas. And I must say he looked fine in those old clothes.'

'Baron Hausberg!' cried Hughie. 'Good heavens! I gave him a pound!' and he sank back into his chair in shock.

'Gave him a pound!' shouted Trevor and he roared with

17

laughter. 'My dear boy, you'll never see it again. His business is with other people's money.'

'I think you ought to have told me, Alan,' said Hughie in a bad temper, 'and not have let me make such a fool of myself.'

'Well, to begin with, Hughie,' said Trevor, 'I never thought that you went about giving your money away in that careless manner. I can understand your kissing a pretty model, but not giving money to an ugly one. Besides, when you came in I didn't know whether Hausberg would like his name mentioned. You know he wasn't in his usual dress!'

'How stupid he must think me!' said Hughie.

'Not at all. He was in the highest spirits after you left, and kept laughing to himself. I couldn't understand why he was so interested in knowing all about you, but I see it all now. He'll keep your pound for you, pay you interest every six months, and have a story to tell after dinner.'

'I am an unlucky devil,' said Hughie. 'The best thing I can do is to go to bed; and, my dear Alan, you mustn't tell anyone. I wouldn't dare show my face if people knew.'

'Nonsense! It shows your kindness of spirit, Hughie. Have another cigarette, and you can talk about Laura as much as you like.'

But Hughie refused to stay; he walked home, feeling very unhappy, and leaving Alan Trevor helpless with laughter.

The next morning, as he was at breakfast, the servant brought him a card on which was written, 'Mr Gustave Naudin, for Baron Hausberg'. 'I suppose he wants me to say I am sorry about yesterday,' said Hughie to himself, and he told the servant to bring the visitor in.

An old gentleman with gold glasses and grey hair came into the room and said, 'Have I the honour of speaking to Mr Erskine?'

Hughie agreed that he was Mr Erskine.

'I have come from Baron Hausberg,' he continued. 'The Baron –'

'I beg, sir, that you will tell him how truly sorry I am,' said Hughie quickly.

'The Baron,' said the old gentleman with a smile, 'has asked me to bring you this letter'; and he held out an envelope.

On the outside was written 'A wedding present to Hugh Erskine and Laura Merton, from an old beggar', and inside was a cheque for ten thousand pounds.

Lord Emsworth and the Girl Friend   *P. G. Wodehouse*

The day was so warm, so fair, so wonderfully a thing of sunshine and blue skies and bird song that anyone who knew Clarence, Lord Emsworth, and knew also his liking for fine weather, would have imagined him going about the place on this summer morning with a bright smile and a happy heart. Instead of this, bent over the breakfast table, he was directing a look of violent hatred at a blameless fish on his plate. It was August Bank Holiday,★ and Blandings Castle on August Bank Holiday became, in his lordship's opinion, unbearable.

This was the day when his park and grounds were filled with tents, toys, balls and paper bags; when a wave of farm workers and their crying children swallowed up those places of ancient peace. On August Bank Holiday he was not allowed to wander around his gardens in an old coat: he was made to dress like a gentleman and told to go out and be pleasant to the people. And in the cool of the quiet evening the same forces put him on a platform and made him give a speech. To a man with a day like that in front of him, fine weather was a bad joke.

His sister, Lady Constance Keeble, looked brightly at him over the coffeepot. 'What a lovely morning!' she said.

Lord Emsworth's misery deepened. He disliked being asked – by this woman of all women – to behave as if everything was for the best in this best of all possible worlds.

'Have you got your speech ready?'

'Yes.'

'Well, make sure you learn it by heart this time and don't keep stopping like you did last year.'

★ Bank Holidays are official holidays when banks and most businesses are closed.

Lord Emsworth pushed his fish away. He had lost his desire for food.

'And don't forget you have to go to the village this morning to judge the garden competition.'

'All right,' said his lordship bad-temperedly. 'I've not forgotten.'

'I think I will come to the village with you. There are a number of London children here at the moment on a Fresh Air visit, and I must warn them to behave properly when they come to the Fête this afternoon. You know what London children are. McAllister says he found one of them in the gardens the other day, picking his flowers.'

At any other time the news of this behaviour would, no doubt, have affected Lord Emsworth deeply. But now his self-pity was so great that he did not even reply. He drank his coffee in the manner of a man who wished it was poison.

'By the way,' said Lady Constance. 'McAllister was speaking to me last night about that new path through the trees. He seems to want it very much.'

'Glug!' said Lord Emsworth – which, as any student of language will tell you, is the sound which all lords make when struck to the soul while drinking coffee.

Concerning Glasgow, that great business and industrial city in Scotland, much has been written. The only thing about it which concerns the present writer, though, is the fact that its citizens are often cold, silent men who know what they want and intend to get it. Such a man was Angus McAllister, head gardener at Blandings Castle.

For years Angus McAllister had had as his chief desire the building of a path through a particularly famous group of the Castle's trees. For years he had been bringing this plan to the notice of his employer, though a man from any other city would have been made uncomfortable by Lord Emsworth's obvious dislike of the whole idea. And now, it seemed, the gardener had brought up the subject again.

'Path through the trees!' Lord Emsworth stiffened through the whole length of his thin body. Nature, he had always said, intended the ground under the trees to be covered with grass. And, whatever Nature felt about it, he personally was not going to have men with Glasgow speech patterns, and faces like drunken potatoes, coming along and spoiling that lovely stretch of green. 'Path! Why not a few boards with advertisements on them and a petrol pump? That's what the man would really like.'

'Well, I think it is a good idea,' said his sister. 'One could walk there in wet weather then. Wet grass is terribly bad for shoes.'

Lord Emsworth rose. He could bear no more of this. He left the table, the room and the house and, reaching these particular trees some minutes later, was disgusted to find that Angus McAllister was there in person. The head gardener was standing looking at the grass like a high priest of some ancient religion about to kill a human being for the gods.

'Morning, McAllister,' said Lord Emsworth coldly.

'Good morrrrning, your lordship.'

There was a pause. Angus McAllister, stretching out a foot, pressed it into the grass. The meaning of this movement was plain. It showed a general dislike of grass: and Lord Emsworth looked at the man unpleasantly through his glasses. Though he did not often think about religion, he was wondering why Chance, if forced to produce head gardeners, had found it necessary to make them so Scottish. In the case of McAllister, why had it been necessary to make him a human being at all? He felt that he might have liked McAllister if he had been some sort of animal – a dog, perhaps.

'I was speaking to her ladyship yesterday.'

'Oh?'

'About the path. Her ladyship likes the idea a lot.'

'Really! Well ...'

Lord Emsworth's face had turned bright pink, and he was about to speak the violent words which were forming in his mind when suddenly he noticed the expression in the head gardener's eye and paused. Angus McAllister was looking at him, and he knew what that look meant. Just one word, his eye was saying – in Scottish, of course – just one word out of you and I will leave. And with a sickening shock Lord Emsworth realized how completely he was in this man's power.

He moved his feet miserably. Yes, he was helpless. Except for that idea about the path. Angus McAllister was a head gardener in a thousand, and he needed him. That, unfortunately, had been proved by experience. Once before, when they were growing for the flower show a plant which had later won first prize, he had dared to ignore McAllister's advice. And Angus had left, and he had been forced to beg – yes, to beg – him to come back. An employer cannot hope to do this sort of thing and still rule with an iron hand. Filled with the kind of anger which dares to burn but does not dare to show itself, Lord Emsworth coughed.

'I'll – er – I'll think it over, McAllister.'

'Mphm.'

'I have to go to the village now. I will see you later.'

'Mphm.'

'I will – er – think it over.'

'Mphm.'

♦

The job of judging the flowers in the garden competition of the little village of Blandings Parva was one which Lord Emsworth had looked forward to with pleasure. But now, even though he had managed to escape from his sister Constance, he came to the duty with an unhappy spirit. It is always unpleasant for a proud man to realize that he is no longer captain of his soul; that he is in fact under the big boots of a head gardener from Glasgow; and, thinking about this, he judged the gardens without paying much attention to them. It was only when he came to the last on his list that he saw something that attracted his attention.

This, he saw, looking over its broken fence, was not at all a bad little garden. He opened the gate and wandered in. And a sleeping dog opened one eye and looked at him. It was one of those very ordinary, hairy dogs, and its look was cold and distrustful, like that of a businessman who thinks someone is going to play a trick on him.

Lord Emsworth did not see the animal. He had wandered over to some flowers and now, bending down, he smelt them.

The dog for some reason appeared to think that this action was criminal, and jumped up to defend his home. The next moment the world had become full of terrible noises, and Lord Emsworth's worries were swept away in a strong desire to save his legs from harm.

He was not at his best with strange dogs. Except for saying 'Go away, sir!' and jumping about in a surprisingly active way for a man of his age, he had done little to defend himself when the house door opened and a girl came out.

'Hoy!' cried the girl.

And immediately, at the sound of her voice, the dog, stopping the attack, ran towards the newcomer and lay on his back at her feet with all four legs in the air. The sight reminded Lord Emsworth of his own behaviour when in the presence of Angus McAllister.

He looked at the person who had saved him. She was a small girl, of uncertain age – possibly twelve or thirteen, though a combination of London weather and a hard life had given her face a sort of lined motherliness which caused his lordship to treat her as someone of his own age. She was the kind of girl you see carrying a baby nearly as large as herself and still with enough strength to lead one little brother by the hand and shout at another in the distance. Her face shone from recent soaping, and she was wearing her best dress. She wore her hair pulled tightly back from her face.

'Er – thank you,' said Lord Emsworth.

'Thank you, sir,' said the girl.

What she was thanking him for, his lordship was not able to understand. Later, when they knew each other better, he discovered that this strange gratitude was a habit with his new friend. She thanked everybody for everything. At the moment, the habit surprised him.

Lack of practice had made it a little difficult for Lord Emsworth to talk to members of the opposite sex. He tried hard to think of a subject.

'Fine day.'

'Yes, sir. Thank you, sir.'

'Are you' – Lord Emsworth secretly looked at his list – 'are you the daughter of – er – Ebenezer Sprockett?' he asked, thinking, as he had often thought before, what ugly names some of the people who lived on his lands possessed.

'No, sir. I'm from London, sir.'

'Ah? London, eh? Rather warm it must be there.' He paused. Then, remembering his youth: 'Er – been to many dances this season?'

'No, sir.'

'Everybody out of London now, I suppose? What's your name?'

'Gladys, sir. Thank you, sir. This is Ern.'

A small boy had wandered out of the small house, a rather angry-looking boy, bearing surprisingly in his hand a large and beautiful bunch of flowers. Lord Emsworth smiled politely and with the addition of this third person to the conversation felt more comfortable.

'How do you do?' he said. 'What pretty flowers!'

With her brother's arrival, Gladys had also felt happier.

'Good, aren't they?' she agreed eagerly. 'I got 'em for 'im up at the big house. Ooh! The man the place belongs to ran after me! 'E found me picking them, and 'e shouted something and came runnin' after me, but I threw a stone at 'im, and 'e stopped to rub his leg and I came away.'

Lord Emsworth could have corrected her idea that Blandings Castle and its gardens belonged to Angus McAllister, but his mind was so filled with admiration and gratitude that he did not do so. He looked at the girl respectfully. This wonderful woman was able to control dogs with just a word, and actually threw stones at Angus McAllister – a thing which he had never had courage to do himself in their nine years together – and, what was more, hit him on the leg with them.

'Ern,' said Gladys, changing the subject, 'is wearing hair oil today.'

Lord Emsworth had already noticed this, and had, in fact, been moving away as she spoke.

'For the Feet,' explained Gladys.

'The feet? Oh, you are going to the Fête?'

'Yes, sir, thank you, sir.'

For the first time Lord Emsworth began to think of the event with something like pleasure.

'We must look for each other there,' he said kindly. 'You will remember me again? I shall be wearing' – he swallowed – 'a top hat.'

'Ern's going to wear a straw hat that's been given 'im.'

Lord Emsworth looked at the lucky young devil with a feeling of jealousy. He thought he knew that straw hat. It had been his companion for about six years and then had been torn from him by his sister Constance and given away.

He thought sadly about the lost hat.

26

'Well, goodbye.'

'Goodbye, sir. Thank you, sir.'

Lord Emsworth walked thoughtfully out of the garden and, turning into the little street, met Lady Constance.

'Oh, there you are, Clarence.'

'Yes,' said Lord Emsworth, since it was true.

'Have you finished judging the gardens?'

'Yes.'

'I am just going into this last house here. I am told there is a little girl from London staying there. I want to warn her to behave properly this afternoon. I have spoken to the others.'

Lord Emsworth stood up straight. His glasses were not level, but in spite of this he looked commanding.

'Well, be careful what you say,' he ordered.

'What do you mean?'

'You know what I mean. I have the greatest respect for the young lady of whom you speak. She behaved on a certain recent occasion – on two recent occasions – with courage and skill, and I won't have her spoken to severely. Understand that!'

◆

The real title of the party which was held every year on the first Monday in August in the park of Blandings Castle was the Blandings Parva School Treat; and it seemed to Lord Emsworth, watching the event from under the shadow of his tall black hat, that if this was the sort of thing schools enjoyed, he and they enjoyed very different things.

The sheep and cows to whom this park usually belonged had been sent away to places unknown, leaving the grass to children whose activity frightened Lord Emsworth, and to adults who appeared to have lost all their self-respect. Look at Mrs Rossiter over there, for example. On any other day of the year, when you met her, Mrs Rossiter was a nice, quiet woman who smiled

27

respectfully as you passed. Today, red in the face and with her hat on one side, she seemed to have gone completely mad. She was wandering here and there drinking out of a bottle; and when she was not drinking, she was using her mouth to blow through some child's toy and make a terrible noise.

The injustice of the thing hurt Lord Emsworth. This park was his own private park. What right had people to come and make noises in it? How would Mrs Rossiter like it if one afternoon he suddenly marched into her neat little garden in the High Street and rushed about over her grass making noises?

And it was always on these occasions so terribly hot. Even if July ended with snow, as soon as the first Monday in August arrived and he had to put on a stiff collar, out came the burning sun.

Of course, admitted Lord Emsworth, since he was a fair man, this worked both ways. The hotter the day, the more quickly his collar melted and stopped cutting into his neck. This afternoon, for example, the collar had almost immediately become something like a wet cloth.

A masterful figure came to his side.

'Clarence!'

Lord Emsworth's spiritual state was now such that not even the arrival of his sister Constance could add much to his discomfort.

'Clarence, you look a terrible sight.'

'I know I do. Who wouldn't, in clothes like these?'

'Please don't be childish, Clarence. I cannot understand why you hate dressing for once in your life like a reasonable English gentleman, and not like a beggar.'

'It's this top hat. It's exciting the children.'

'What on earth do you mean, exciting the children?'

'Well, all I can tell you is that just now, as I was passing the place where they're playing football – football! In weather like this! – a small boy called out something insulting and threw a nut at it.'

'If you will tell me which boy it was,' said Lady Constance, angrily, 'I will have him severely punished.'

'How,' replied his lordship, equally angry, 'can I do that? They all look alike to me. And if I knew him, I would shake him by the hand. A boy who throws nuts at top hats is in his right mind. And stiff collars ...'

'Stiff! That's what I came to speak to you about. Do you know what your collar looks like? Go in and change it immediately.'

'But, my dear Constance ...'

'Immediately, Clarence. I simply cannot understand a man having so little pride in his appearance. But all your life you have been like that. I remember when we were children ...'

Lord Emsworth's past was not so pure that he was prepared to stand and listen to an account of it by a sister with a good memory.

'Oh, all right, all right, all right,' he said. 'I'll change it, I'll change it.'

'Well, hurry. They are just starting tea.'

Lord Emsworth trembled.

'Have I got to go into that tea tent?'

'Of course you have. As master of Blandings Castle ...'

A bitter laugh from the poor creature she was describing drowned the rest of the sentence.

◆

It always seemed to Lord Emsworth, in examining these entertainments, that the show on August Bank Holiday at Blandings Castle reached its lowest point when tea was served in the big tent. When tea was over, the pain grew less, though it became worse again at the moment when he stepped to the edge of the platform and cleared his throat and tried to remember

29

what on earth he had planned to say. After that the pain disappeared again until the following August.

The tent had stood all day under a burning sun, and conditions during the tea hour were such that they could not have been more unpleasant. Lord Emsworth was late, delayed by the necessary change to his collar. He entered the tent when the meal was half over, and was pleased to find that his second collar began to lose its stiffness almost immediately. But that was the only touch of happiness that was given to him. As soon as he was in the tent, it took his experienced eye only a moment to see that the present meal was even more terrible than those that had gone before.

The young people of Blandings Parva were not known as troublemakers. In all villages, of course, there must be violent characters – in Blandings Parva the names of Willie Drake and Thomas Blenkiron come immediately to mind – but on the whole the local youth could be controlled. It was the addition of the Fresh Air London visitors which gave the present meeting its violent nature.

The London child has a confidence which his country cousin lacks. Years of sharp replies to angry parents and relatives have cured him of any shyness, with the result that when he wants anything he takes it, and when he is amused by anything unusual in the personal appearance of members of the governing classes, he finds no difficulty in saying so openly. Already, up and down the long tables, the front teeth of one of the schoolteachers were being loudly discussed. Lord Emsworth was not usually a man of quick thought, but it seemed to him at this moment that it would be wise to take off his top hat before his little guests noticed it.

The action was not, in the end, necessary. As he raised his hand to take it off, a small, hard cake, flying through the air, took it off for him.

Lord Emsworth had had enough. Even Constance, an

unreasonable woman, could not expect him to stay and smile in conditions like these. Lord Emsworth went slowly towards the way out, and left.

◆

Outside the tent the world was quieter, but only slightly quieter. What Lord Emsworth wanted was to be alone, and in all the broad park there seemed to be only one spot where he could be alone. This was a red-roofed hut, used in happier times by cows. Hurrying there, his lordship was just beginning to enjoy the cool darkness of the inside of the hut when from one of the dark corners, causing him to jump and bite his tongue, there came a small sound.

He turned. This was too much. With the whole park to go to, why should a child come in here? He spoke angrily.

'Who's that?'

'Me, sir. Thank you, sir.'

Only one person whom Lord Emsworth knew was able to thank him for having been spoken to so sharply. His anger died away. He felt like a man who, by mistake, has kicked a loyal dog.

'Good heavens!' he cried. 'What in the world are you doing here?'

'Please, sir, I was put 'ere.'

'Put? What do you mean, put? Why?'

'For stealing things, sir.'

'Eh? What? Stealing things? Most strange. What did you steal?'

'Two sandwiches, two apples and a piece of cake.'

The girl had come out of her corner. Force of habit had made her give the list of what she had stolen in the same flat voice as she used at school to her teacher, but Lord Emsworth could see that she was very upset. Tears shone on her face, and no Emsworth had ever been able to watch a woman's tears. He was deeply troubled.

He gave her his handkerchief.

'Thank you, sir.'

'What did you say you had taken?'

She told him again.

'Did you eat them?'

'No, sir. They weren't for me. They were for Ern.'

'Ern? Oh, yes. Of course. For Ern?'

'Yes, sir.'

'But why on earth couldn't Ern have – er – stolen them for himself? He's a strong young boy.'

'Ern wasn't allowed to come, sir.'

'What? Not allowed? Who said he mustn't?'

'The lady, sir.'

'What lady?'

'The one that came in just after you'd gone this morning.'

An angry cry escaped from Lord Emsworth's lips. Constance! What did Constance mean by changing his list of guests without asking him? Constance, eh? One of these days Constance would go too far.

'Terrible!' he cried.

'Yes, sir.'

'Did she give any reason?'

'The lady didn't like Ern biting 'er in the leg, sir.'

'Ern bit her in the leg?'

'Yes, sir. Pretending to be a dog, sir, 'e was. And the lady was cross and Ern wasn't allowed to come, and I told him I'd bring him back something nice.'

Lord Emsworth breathed heavily. He had not supposed that a family like this existed. The sister threw stones at Angus McAllister, the brother bit Constance in the leg . . . It was too wonderful to be true!

'I thought if I 'ad nothing myself, it would make it all right.'

'Nothing?' Lord Emsworth was astonished. 'Do you mean to tell me you have not had tea?'

'No, sir. Thank you, sir. I thought if I 'ad none, then it would be all right if Ern 'ad what I would 'ave 'ad.'

His lordship's head, never very strong, swam a little in confusion. Then he understood. 'Good heavens!' he said. 'I never heard anything so terrible in my life. Come with me immediately.'

'The lady said I had to stop 'ere, sir.'

'Never mind the lady!' Lord Emsworth commanded.

'Thank you, sir.'

Five minutes later Beach, Lord Emsworth's manservant, enjoying a short sleep in the housekeeper's room, was awakened by the unexpected ringing of a bell. Answering its call, he found his employer in the library, and with him a surprising young person.

'Beach!'

'Your lordship?'

'This young lady would like some tea.'

'Very good, your lordship.'

'Sandwiches, you know, and apples and cake, and that sort of thing.'

'Very good, your lordship.'

'And she has a brother, Beach.'

'Really, your lordship?'

'She will want to take some food away for him.' Lord Emsworth turned to his guest. 'Ernest would like a little chicken, perhaps?'

'Ooooh!'

'I beg your pardon?'

'Yes, sir. Thank you, sir.'

'Fine! Then bring a bottle of that new wine, Beach. It's some they sent me to try,' explained his lordship. 'Nothing special, you understand,' he added, 'but quite good. Put all that together in a package, Beach, and leave it on the table in the hall. We will pick it up as we go out.'

It was less hot when Lord Emsworth and his guest came out of the great door of the castle into the evening air. Gladys, holding her host's hand and the package, was happy. She had had a good tea. Life seemed to have nothing more to offer.

Lord Emsworth did not share this view. He was ready to do more.

'Now, is there anything else you can think of that Ernest would like?' he asked. 'If so, just say so. Beach, can you think of anything?'

Beach was unable to do so.

'No, your lordship. I added – on my own responsibility, your lordship – some hard-boiled eggs.'

'Excellent! You're sure there is nothing else?'

A hopeful look came into Gladys's eyes.

'Could he have some flarze?'

'Certainly,' said Lord Emsworth. 'Certainly, certainly, certainly. Of course. Just what I was going to suggest – er – what *is* flarze?'

Beach explained.

'I think the young lady means flowers, your lordship.'

'Yes, sir. Thank you, sir. Flarze.'

'Oh?' said Lord Emsworth. 'Oh? Flowers?' he said slowly.

He took off his glasses, cleaned them thoughtfully, put them on again and looked out at the gardens. They contained thousands of flowers. They were bright with flowers of all kinds. But what about Angus McAllister? What would he do if they were picked?

As a general rule, the way to get flowers out of Angus McAllister was as follows. You waited until he was feeling kind-hearted, which happened rarely. Then you led the conversation gently round to the subject of flower arrangements. Then, at the right moment, you asked if he could possibly let you have a few. The last thing you thought of doing was to start picking the flowers yourself.

'I – er . . .' said Lord Emsworth.

He stopped. He suddenly saw himself as he was: the unspeakably weak representative of a family which in the old days had certainly known how to treat its employees. Long ago, people had known how to speak to servants. Of course, they had possessed certain advantages which he lacked. If they got angry with a head gardener, they had him cut to pieces, and no questions were asked – but in spite of this, he realized that they were better men than he was, and that if he allowed fear of Angus McAllister to prevent this charming girl and her brother from having flowers, he had no right to call himself Lord Emsworth.

Lord Emsworth struggled with his fears.

'Certainly, certainly, certainly,' he said. 'Take as many as you want.'

And so it happened that Angus McAllister's eyes fell on a sight which first froze his blood and then caused it to boil. Moving here and there through his gardens was a small girl picking his flowers. And – this made his blood boil – it was the same girl who two days ago had thrown stones at him and hit him on the leg. The quietness of the summer evening was broken by a noise that sounded like boilers exploding, and Angus came towards her at 45 miles an hour.

Gladys did not wait. She was a London child, trained from a young age to be brave in times of danger, but this attack was so sudden that for a moment it broke her nerve. With a frightened cry she ran to where Lord Emsworth stood, and hid behind him.

Lord Emsworth was not feeling very good himself. We have pictured him a few moments ago deciding to put McAllister in his proper place. But truth forces us to admit that this decision was taken because he believed the head gardener to be a quarter of a mile away. Lord Emsworth's knees shook, and the soul within him trembled.

And then something happened and the whole situation changed.

It was, in itself, a small thing, but it served to encourage Lord Emsworth. What happened was that Gladys, needing further protection, slid a small, hot hand into his.

She trusted him.

'He's coming,' whispered a small voice inside Lord Emsworth.

'What about it?' replied Lord Emsworth bravely.

'Put him in his place,' breathed his lordship's great-grandfathers.

'I will,' replied Lord Emsworth.

He stood up straight. He felt masterful. If the man decided to leave his job, let him.

'Well, McAllister?' said Lord Emsworth coldly.

He took off his top hat and brushed it against his coat.

'What is the matter, McAllister?'

He put his top hat on again.

'You appear to be upset, McAllister.'

He moved his head. The hat fell off. He let it lie. Free from its hateful weight, he felt more masterful than ever.

'This young lady,' said Lord Emsworth, 'has my full permission to pick all the flowers she wants, McAllister. If you do not agree with me in this matter, McAllister, say so and we will discuss what you are going to do about it, McAllister. These gardens, McAllister, belong to me, and if you do not realize the fact you will, no doubt be able to find another employer with more – er – sympathy for your views. I value your services highly, McAllister, but I will not be ordered about in my own garden, McAllister.'

A long moment followed in which Nature stood still, breathless. All the flowers stood still. From far off in the direction of the park there sounded the happy cries of children, who were probably breaking things, but even these seemed quieter than before.

Angus McAllister stood red and angry in the face. He was confused. Angus had never thought that his employer would suggest that he might look for another position. And now that he had suggested it, Angus McAllister disliked the idea very much. He loved Blandings Castle. He would be miserable anywhere else. He made his decision.

'Mphm,' said Angus McAllister.

'Oh, and by the way, McAllister,' said Lord Emsworth, 'that matter about the path through the trees. I've been thinking it over, and I won't have it. Certainly not. Spoil my beautiful gardens with an ugly path? Ruin the most beautiful spot in one of the finest and oldest gardens in England? Certainly not. No. Try to remember, McAllister, as you work in the gardens of Blandings Castle, that you are not back in Scotland, laying out playing fields. That is all, McAllister; that is all.'

'Mphm,' said Angus McAllister.

He turned. He walked away. He disappeared. Nature began to breathe again. The wind began to blow. And all over the gardens, the birds, which had stopped singing, began again.

Lord Emsworth took out his handkerchief and ran it over his face. He was shaken, but a new sense of being a man among men filled him with pleasure. He almost wished that his sister Constance would come along and say something while he felt like this.

He had his wish.

'Clarence!'

Yes, there she was, hurrying towards him up the garden path. She, like McAllister, seemed upset. Something was on her mind.

'Clarence!'

'Don't keep saying "Clarence!"' said Lord Emsworth with his head held high. 'What on earth is the matter, Constance?'

'Matter? Do you know what the time is? Do you know that everybody is waiting down there for you to make your speech?'

Lord Emsworth looked her in the eye severely.

'I do not,' he said. 'And I don't care. I'm not going to make any speech. If you want a speech, let someone else make it. Or make it yourself. Speech! I never heard such nonsense in my life.' He turned to Gladys. 'Now, my dear,' he said, 'if you will just give me time to get out of these terrible clothes and this devilish collar and put on something human, we'll go down to the village and have a talk with Ern.'

The Doll's House   *Katherine Mansfield*

When dear old Mrs Hay went back to London after staying with the Burnells, she sent the children a doll's house. It was so big that it had to be left in the courtyard, and there it stayed on two wooden boxes. No harm could come to it; it was summer. And perhaps the smell of paint would have gone off by the time it had to be taken in. For, really, the smell of paint coming from that doll's house was quite enough to make anyone seriously ill, in Aunt Beryl's opinion.

There stood the doll's house, a dark, oily green. Its two solid little chimneys, fixed to the roof, were painted red and white, and the door was yellow. Four windows, real windows, were divided into four again by broad lines of green.

The perfect, perfect little house! Who could possibly object to the smell? It was part of the joy, part of the newness.

'Open it quickly, someone!'

The hook at the side was stuck. Pat opened it with his knife and the whole house front swung back, and – there you were, looking at one and the same moment into the sitting room and dining room, the kitchen and two bedrooms. That is the way for a house to open! Why don't all houses open like that? How much more exciting than looking through a half-open door like that? How much more exciting than looking through a half-open door into a little hall! That is – isn't it – what you want to know about a house when you come to the door?

The Burnell children thought it was wonderful; they had never seen anything like it in their lives. There was wallpaper on the walls. There were pictures on the walls, painted on the paper, complete with gold frames. All the floors were red except in the kitchen; red chairs in the sitting room, green in the dining room;

tables, beds with real bedclothes, furniture, little plates. But what Kezia liked more than anything was the lamp. It stood in the middle of the dining-room table, a beautiful yellow lamp with white glass over it. It was even filled all ready for lighting, though, of course, you couldn't light it. But there was something inside that looked like oil and moved when you shook it.

The father and mother dolls, who lay very stiff in the sitting room, and their two children asleep upstairs, were really too big for the doll's house. They didn't look as though they belonged. But the lamp was perfect. It seemed to smile at Kezia, to say, 'I live here.' The lamp was real.

The Burnell children could hardly walk to school fast enough the next morning.

'I must tell,' said Isabel, 'because I'm the oldest. And you two can join in after. But I must tell first.'

Isabel always gave orders, but she was always right, and Lottie and Kezia knew too well the powers that went with being oldest. They walked through the thick flowers at the edge of the road and said nothing.

'And I must choose who's to come and see it first. Mother said I could.'

It had been arranged that while the doll's house stood in the courtyard they could ask the girls at school, two at a time, to come and look. Not to stay to tea, of course, or to come wandering through the house. But just to stand quietly in the courtyard while Isabel showed them the attractions of the doll's house, and Lottie and Kezia looked pleased.

But although they hurried, by the time they had reached the fence of the boys' playground the bell had begun to ring. They only just had time to take off their hats and get into line before their names were called. Never mind. Isabel tried to look very important and whispered behind her hand to the girls near her, 'I've got something to tell you at playtime.'

Playtime came and Isabel was surrounded. The girls of her class nearly fought to put their arms around her, to walk away with her, to be her special friend. She received them like a queen under the great trees at the side of the playground. Laughing together, the little girls pressed close to her. And the only two who stayed outside the ring were the two who were always outside, the little Kelveys. They knew that they must not come anywhere near the Burnells.

The fact was, the school the Burnell children went to was not the kind of place their parents would have chosen if there had been a choice. But it was the only school for miles. And the result was that all the children of the neighbourhood, the judge's little girls, the doctor's daughters, the shopkeeper's children, the milkman's, were forced to mix together. There was an equal number of rough little boys as well. But some children could never become friends; there was a limit. The line was drawn at the Kelveys. Many of the children, including the Burnells, were not allowed even to speak to them. They walked past the Kelveys with their heads in the air, and as the other children always copied what the Burnells did, the Kelveys were avoided by everybody. Even the teacher had a special voice for them, and a special smile for the other children when Lil Kelvey came up to her desk with a bunch of cheap-looking flowers.

They were the daughters of a hard-working little washerwoman, who went from house to house. This was bad enough. But where was Mr Kelvey? No one knew. But everybody said he was in prison. So they were the daughters of a washerwoman and a criminal. Very nice company for other people's children! And they looked it! Why Mrs Kelvey made them wear such strange clothes was hard to understand. The truth was they were dressed in 'bits' given to her by the people for whom she worked. Lil, for example, who was a fat, plain child, came to school in a dress made from a green tablecloth of the Burnells', with red arms from the Logans' curtains. Her hat, resting on top of her high forehead, was a grown-up woman's hat, once the property of Miss Lecky, the postmistress. It was turned up at the back. How silly she looked! It was impossible not to laugh. And her little sister, Else, wore a long white dress, rather like a nightdress, and a pair of little boy's boots. But whatever Else wore, she would have looked strange. She was a very small child, with short hair and big, sad eyes. Nobody had ever seen her smile; she hardly ever spoke. She went through life holding on to Lil, with a piece of Lil's dress between her fingers. Where Lil went, Else followed. In the playground, on the road going to and from school, there was Lil marching in front and Else holding on behind. Only when she wanted anything, or when she was out of breath, Else gave Lil a pull, and Lil stopped. The Kelveys never failed to understand each other.

Now they waited at the edge; you couldn't stop them listening. When the little girls turned round and laughed at them, Lil, as usual, gave her silly, embarrassed smile, but Else only looked.

And Isabel's voice, so very proud, went on telling about the doll's house. The coloured chairs caused great excitement, but so did the beds with real bedclothes.

When she finished, Kezia added, 'You've forgotten the lamp, Isabel.'

'Oh, yes,' said Isabel, 'and there's a little lamp, made of yellow glass, with a white top, that stands on the dining room table. It's just like a real one.'

'The lamp's best of all,' cried Kezia. She thought Isabel wasn't saying enough about the little lamp. But nobody paid any attention. Isabel was choosing the two who would come back with them that afternoon and see it. She chose Emmie Cole and Lena Logan. But when the others knew that they were all going to have a chance to see it, they couldn't be nice enough to Isabel. One by one they put their arms around Isabel and walked away with her.

Only the little Kelveys moved away, forgotten; there was nothing more for them to hear.

Days passed, and as more children saw the doll's house, the fame of it spread. It became the one subject of talk. The one question was, 'Have you seen the Burnells' doll's house? Oh, isn't it lovely!' 'Haven't you seen it? Oh, dear!'

Even the dinner hour was given up to talking about it. The little girls sat under the trees eating their lunch, while always, as near as they could get, sat the Kelveys, Else holding on to Lil, listening too.

'Mother,' said Kezia, 'can't I ask the Kelveys just once?'

'Certainly not, Kezia.'

'But why not?'

'Run away, Kezia; you know quite well why not.'

At last everybody had seen it except them. On that day they were all rather tired of the subject. It was the dinner hour. The children stood together under the trees, and suddenly, as they looked at the Kelveys eating out of their paper, always by themselves, always listening, they wanted to hurt them. Emmie Cole started the whisper.

'Lil Kelvey's going to be a servant when she grows up.'

'O-oh, how terrible!' said Isabel Burnell, looking Emmie in the eye.

Emmie swallowed in a very special way and looked at Isabel as she'd seen her mother do on those occasions.

'It's true – it's true – it's true,' she said.

'Shall I ask her?' Lena Logan whispered.

'You're afraid to,' said Jessie May.

'I'm not frightened,' said Lena. Suddenly she gave a little cry and danced in front of the other girls. 'Watch! Watch me! Watch me now!' said Lena. And slowly, dragging one foot, laughing behind her hand, Lena went over to the Kelveys.

Lil looked up from her dinner. She wrapped the rest quickly away. Else stopped eating. What was coming now?

'Is it true you're going to be a servant when you grow up, Lil Kelvey?' cried Lena at the top of her voice.

Dead silence. But instead of answering, Lil only gave her silly, embarrassed smile. She didn't seem to object to the question at all. What a disappointment for Lena. The girls began to laugh.

Lena couldn't bear that. 'Your father's in prison!' she cried.

This was such a wonderful thing to have said that the little girls rushed away together, deeply, deeply excited, wild with joy. Someone found a long rope and they began jumping over it. And never did they play so happily as on that morning.

In the afternoon Pat came for the Burnell children and took them home. There were visitors. Isabel and Lottie, who liked visitors, went upstairs to change their dresses. But Kezia went secretly out at the back. Nobody was there; she began to swing on the big white gates of the courtyard. Soon, looking along the road, she saw two little dots. They grew bigger; they were coming towards her. Now she could see that one was in front and one close behind. Now she could see that they were the Kelveys. Kezia stopped swinging. She got off the gate as if she was going to run away. Then she waited. The Kelveys came nearer, and beside them walked their shadows, very long, stretching right across the road with their heads in the flowers. Kezia climbed back on the gate; she had made up her mind; she swung out.

'Hullo,' she said to the passing Kelveys.

They were so astonished that they stopped. Lil gave her silly smile. Else just looked at her.

'You can come and see our doll's house if you want to,' said Kezia, and she dragged one toe on the ground. But when she heard that, Lil turned red and shook her head quickly.

'Your mother told our mother you weren't allowed to speak to us.'

'Oh, well,' said Kezia. She didn't know what to reply. 'It doesn't matter. Come on. Nobody's looking.'

But Lil shook her head even harder.

'Don't you want to?' asked Kezia.

Suddenly there was a pull at Lil's dress. She turned round. Else was looking at her with big, begging eyes; she wanted to go. For a moment Lil looked at Else very doubtfully. But then Else pulled her dress again. She started to go forward. Kezia led the way. Like two little lost cats they followed across the courtyard to where the doll's house stood.

'There it is,' said Kezia.

There was a pause. Lil breathed loudly; Else was as still as stone.

'I'll open it for you,' said Kezia kindly. She undid the hook and they looked inside.

'There's the sitting room and the dining room, and that's the –'

'Kezia!'

It was Aunt Beryl's voice. They turned round. At the back door stood Aunt Beryl, looking as if she couldn't believe what she saw.

'How dare you ask the little Kelveys into the courtyard?' said her cold, angry voice. 'You know as well as I do, you're not allowed to talk to them. Run away, children, run away immediately. And don't come back again,' said Aunt Beryl. And she stepped into the yard and sent them away as if they were chickens.

'Away you go immediately!' she called, cold and proud.

They did not need telling twice. Burning with shame, somehow they crossed the big courtyard and went out through the white gate.

'Bad, disobedient little girl!' said Aunt Beryl to Kezia, and she shut the doll's house noisily.

When the Kelveys were well out of sight of the Burnells', they sat down to rest on a big red pipe by the side of the road. Lil's face was still burning; she took off her hat and held it on her knee. Dreamily they looked over the fields, past the stream, to where the Logans' cows stood waiting to be milked. What were their thoughts?

Soon Else moved close to her sister. By now she had forgotten the angry lady. She smiled her rare smile.

'I saw the little lamp,' she said softly.

Then both were silent once more.

X-ing a Paragraph   *Edgar Allan Poe*

As it is well known that the 'wise men' in the Bible came 'from the East', and as Mr Touch-and-go Bullet-head came from the East, Mr Bullet-head was therefore a wise man; and if further proof of the matter is needed, here we have it – Mr B. was an editor. A bad temper was his only weakness; he did not consider his inability ever to change his mind a weakness – it was, he firmly believed, his strong point.

I have shown that Touch-and-go Bullet-head was a wise man; and the only occasion on which he was not wise was when, leaving the proper home for all wise men, the East, he moved to the city of Alexander-the-Great-o-nopolis, or some place of similar name, out West.

But I must be fair, and say that when he made up his mind finally to settle in that town, he thought that no newspaper, and therefore no editor, existed in that particular part of the country. When he started the newspaper which he called the *Teapot*, he expected to have no competition. I feel sure that he would never have thought of going to live in Alexander-the-Great-o-nopolis if he had known that, in Alexander-the-Great-o-nopolis, there lived a gentleman named John Smith (if I rightly remember), who for many years had quietly grown fat editing the *Alexander-the-Great-o-nopolis Daily News*. It was only, therefore, because he was not told about John Smith that Mr Bullet-head found himself in Alex – suppose we call it Nopolis, for short – but as he *did* find himself there, and rather than admit to a mistake, he decided to remain. So he did remain; and he did more. He got out his printing press, rented an office exactly opposite that of the *Daily News*, and the third morning after his arrival saw the appearance of the first number of the *Nopolis Teapot* – as nearly as I can remember, this was the name of the new paper.

The leading article, I must admit, was excellent – and very severe. It was especially bitter about things in general – and as for the editor of the *Daily News*, he was cruelly criticized. Some of Bullet-head's remarks were really so strong that I am astonished that John Smith managed to live through the experience. I cannot hope to give all the *Teapot*'s words exactly, but one paragraph goes like this:

Oh, yes! Oh, we can see! O, no doubt! The editor opposite is such a clever man. Oh dear! Oh goodness! What is the world coming to?

An article as bitter and well-formed as this exploded like a bomb among the peaceful citizens of Nopolis. Groups of excited people met to discuss it on street corners. Everyone waited nervously for John Smith's reply. Next morning it appeared in the *Daily News* as follows:

In the *Teapot* of yesterday we find the words: *Oh*, yes, *Oh*, we can see! *Oh*, no doubt! *Oh*, dear! *Oh*, goodness! Why, the man is all O! That explains why he reasons in a circle, and why there is neither beginning nor end to him, nor to anything he says. We really do not believe the man can write a word that hasn't an O in it. We wonder if this O-ing is a habit of his. He came from the East in a great hurry. We wonder if he OWES as much there as he does here? O, it is pitiful!

I shall not attempt to describe the anger of Mr Bullet-head at these shocking suggestions. he did not seem to be as angry at the attack on his honesty as one would have imagined. It was the attack on his *style* that upset him. What! He, 'Touch-and-go Bullet-head' not able to write a word without an O in it! He would soon show Smith that he was mistaken. Yes! He would let Mr John Smith see that he, Bullet-head, could write a whole paragraph – even a whole article – in which that unfortunate vowel did not once appear. But no! That would be doing just what John Smith wanted. He, Bullet-head, would make *no* change in his style for the satisfaction of Mr Smith in the world. The O for ever! He would keep the O. He would use O whenever he liked.

Burning with this determination, the great Touch-and-go, in the next *Teapot*, came out with this simple paragraph.

The editor of the *Teapot* has the honour of advising the editor of the *Daily News* that he (the *Teapot*) will take an opportunity in tomorrow morning's paper of proving to him (the *Daily News*) that he (the *Teapot*) both can and will be *his own master* in his written style; he (the *Teapot*) will write for the particular satisfaction of him (the *Daily News*) a leading article, of some length, in which the beautiful letter O shall most certainly not be avoided by his (the *Daily News's*) most obedient servant, the *Teapot*.

To carry out this terrible threat which he had made, the great Bullet-head sat up all night until day came, burning the midnight lamp-oil, and busy with the really unequalled paragraph which follows:

So, ho, John! Told you so, you know. Don't shout another time, before you're out of the woods! Does your mother *know* you're out? Oh, no, no! So go home at once, now, John, to your old woods. Go home to your woods – go! You won't? Oh, pooh, pooh, John, don't do so. You've *got* to go, you know. You're only a cow, a poor good-for-nothing-to-nobody dog. Don't complain so, you fool. Oh, John, how you do look! Told you so, you know. Go and drown your sorrows in a bowl!

Tired out, of course, by so wonderful a piece of work, the great Touch-and-go could do nothing more that night. He handed his article to the printer's boy who was waiting, and walked slowly home to bed.

The printer's boy to whom the article was trusted ran upstairs in a great hurry and prepared to set the article in print.

First, of course – as the opening word was 'So' – he looked for and found a capital S. Pleased with this success he immediately threw himself on the box where the little O's were kept – but who can describe his feelings of horror when his fingers came out of it without a letter in them? Who can tell of his astonishment and anger when he realized that the little box was completely empty? Not a single little O was in the little-O box; and, looking fearfully at the capital-O box, he found *that* in exactly the same state – empty. He ran to his master.

'Sir!' said he, breathlessly, 'I can set up nothing without no O's.'

'What do you mean by that?' said the chief, who was very angry at being kept from his bed so late.

'Well, sir, there isn't an O in the office, neither a big one nor a little one!'

'What has happened to all those that were in the box?'

'I don't know, sir,' said the boy, 'but one of those *Daily News* people has been wandering about here, and I expect he's taken every one.'

'I haven't a doubt of it,' replied the chief angrily, turning purple in the face with anger – 'but I tell you what to do, Bob, that's a good boy – you go over to the *Daily News* the first chance you get, and take every one of their I's.'

'Right!' replied Bob. 'I'll go; I'll show them a thing or two. But what about that paragraph? It must go in tonight, you know – if not, there'll be trouble.'

'Trouble enough. Is it a long paragraph, Bob?'

'I shouldn't call it a *very* long paragraph.'

'Ah, well, then! Do the best you can with it! We *must* get it ready,' said the chief, who was buried in work. 'Just put in some other letter for O; nobody's going to read the man's nonsense in any case.'

'Very well,' replied Bob. 'Here I go!' and off he hurried. 'So I have to put out their eyes, do I?' The fact is that, although Bob was only twelve years old and four feet high, he was always ready for a fight.

The difficulty described here happens quite frequently in printing offices; and I cannot explain it, but the fact is certain, that when the difficulty *does* come up, it almost always happens that the letter X is used instead of the letter which is missing. The true reason, perhaps, is that X is the most plentiful letter in the boxes, or it *was* so in old times – for long enough to make the use of it a habit with printers. Bob would have thought it quite wrong to use any other letter than the X.

'I shall have to X this paragraph,' he said to himself, as he read it over in astonishment, 'but it's just about the worst paragraph of O's that I've ever seen.' So he did X the paragraph, and that is how it was printed.

Next morning the population of Nopolis were all astonished to read in the *Teapot* the following leading article:

Sx, hx, Jxhn! Txld yxu sx, yxu knxw. Dxn't shxut anxther time, befxre yxu're xut of the wxxds! Dxes yxur mxther *knxw* yxu're xut? Xh, nx, nx! Sx gx hxme at xnce, nxw, Jxhn, tx yxur xld wxxds. Gx hxme tx yxur wxxds – gx! Yxu wxn't? Xh, pxxh, pxxh, Jxhn, dxn't dx sx. Yxu've *gxt* tx gx, yxu knxw. Sx gx at xnce, and dxn't gx slxw; fxr nxbxdy xwns yxu here, yxu knxw. Yxu're xnly a cxw, a pxxr, gxxd-fxr-nxthing-tx-nxbxdy dxg. Dxn't cxmplain sx, yxu fxxl. Xh, Jxhn, hxw yxu dx lxxk! Txld yxu sx, yxu knxw. Gx and drxwn yxur sxrrxws in a bxwl!

The confusion caused by this strange article cannot be imagined. The first idea in the minds of the population was that some devilish trick was hidden by the signs; and there was a general rush to Bullet-head's house for the purpose of punishing him as he deserved; but that gentleman was nowhere to be found. He had disappeared, no one could tell how; and not even his shadow has ever been seen since.

Unable to find him, people's anger died down at last; but there remained quite a variety of opinions about this unhappy affair.

One gentleman thought the whole thing an X-ellent joke.

Another could only suppose that Bullet-head had decided to X-press his anger in the most imaginative way that he could.

'And to set an X-ample to our children,' suggested another.

It was clear to all that Bullet-head had been driven to X-treme action; and in fact, since *that* editor could not be found, there was some talk of punishing the other one.

The more common feeling, though, was that the affair was simply impossible to X-plain. Nobody could understand what had happened.

The opinion of Bob, the printer's boy (who said nothing about his having X-ed the paragraph), did not receive as much attention as I think it deserved. He said that he had no doubt about the matter at all, that it was a clear case, that Mr Bullet-head never *could* be persuaded to drink like other people, but drank beer all the time, which filled him with wind and made him X (cross) in the X-treme.

The Courtship of Susan Bell   *Anthony Trollope*

John Munroe Bell had been a lawyer in Albany, State of New York, and had been successful. He had been successful as long as success on this earth had been allowed to him. But God had shortened his life.

In his youth he had married a gentle, nervous, pretty, good little wife, whose whole heart and mind had been directed towards doing what he ordered and deserving his love. She had not only deserved it, but had possessed it, and as long as John Munroe Bell had lived, Henrietta Bell – Hetta as he called her – had been a woman who was rich in blessings. After 12 years of such blessings he had died, and had left her with two daughters, a second Hetta and the chief character of our little story, Susan Bell.

A lawyer in Albany may succeed quite well for eight or ten years and still not leave behind him any very large sum of money if he dies at the end of that time. John Bell had saved a few thousand dollars, so that his wife and daughters were left with something, though not a lot.

In those happy days when money had begun to flow in to the young father of the family, he had decided to build for himself, or rather for his young daughters, a small neat house near Saratoga Springs. He filled the house with nice furniture, and then during the summer weeks his wife lived there, and sometimes he rented it out.

I need not tell of the wife's sorrow when the lord of her heart and master of her mind was laid in the grave. At the time of which I am about to speak, it had already been ten years since his death, and her children had grown to be young women beside her. Since that sad day on which they had left Albany, they had lived together at the small house at the Springs. In winter their life had been lonely enough; but as soon as the hot weather began to drive the fainting citizens out of New York, they had always received two or three paying guests – old ladies, usually, and occasionally an old gentleman – persons of steady habits, who liked the women's charges better than they liked the charges of a hotel.

The world knows well enough that Saratoga is a good place to be in July, August and September. It is a very nice place for girls whose fathers' pockets are full of money. Dancing and lovemaking come naturally, and marriage follows only too quickly. But the place was not very happy for Hetta or Susan Bell.

First, their mother was not a courageous woman, and among other anxieties she feared greatly that she would be thought guilty of trying to trap men into marriage. Poor mothers! How often people think they are doing this when they only want their children to be respected like all the others. She feared love too, though she wanted as well as feared it – for her girls, I mean; all such feelings for herself were long ago forgotten. And then she had other fears, and among them was a terror that those girls of hers would be left without husbands. But the result of so many fears and so little money was that Hetta and Susan Bell led dull lives.

I am limited in the number of my pages; if I were not, I would describe completely the qualities and beauties of Hetta and Susan Bell. Here I can say only a few words. At this time of their lives Hetta was nearly twenty-one and Susan was just nineteen. Hetta was a short, rather heavy young woman, with the softest smooth hair, and the brownest bright eyes. She was very useful in the house, good at making cakes; and she thought a great deal, especially in recent months, about he religious duties. Her sister sometimes laughed at the patience with which she listened to the long speeches of Mr Phineas Beckard, a minister of religion. Now, Mr Phineas Beckard was not married.

Susan was not so good a girl in the kitchen or in the house as her sister was, but she was bright in the sitting room. And if her greatest secret were known, it might have been found that Susan was loved a little more. She was taller than her sister; her eyes were blue, as were her mother's; her hair was brighter than Hetta's, but not always so neat. And oh, such a mouth! There; I am allowed no more pages for this.

One very cold winter's day there came a knocking at the door – a young man. In these days there was not often much to upset the calmness of Mrs Bell's house; but on this day there came a knocking at the door – a young man.

Mrs Bell kept an old servant, who had lived with them in those happy Albany days. Her name was Kate O'Brien. She was a large, noisy, good-tempered old Irishwoman, who had joined the family when Mrs Bell first began housekeeping; and, recognizing when she was in a comfortable place, she had remained with them ever since. She had known Hetta as a baby and had been there when Susan was born.

'And what do you want, sir?' said Kate O'Brien, not very pleased as she opened the door and let in all the cold air.

'I wish to see Mrs Bell. Is this not Mrs Bell's house?' said the young man, shaking the snow from his coat.

He did see Mrs Bell, and we will now tell who he was, and why he had come, and how his bag was brought to the house and one of the front bedrooms was prepared for him, and that he drank tea that night in the sitting room.

His name was Aaron Dunn, and by profession he was an engineer. I never quite understood what problem there was with the railway which runs from Schenectady to Lake Champlain in those days of cold and snow. Banks and bridges had in some way suffered, and it was Aaron Dunn's duty to see that they were repaired. Saratoga Springs was at the centre of these misfortunes, and therefore it was necessary that he should stay at Saratoga Springs.

There was at that time in New York City a Mr Bell, great in railway matters – an uncle of the now dead Albany lawyer. He was a rich man, but he liked his riches himself; he did not feel he ought to share them with the wife and daughters of his brother's son. But when Aaron Dunn was sent to Saratoga, he took the young man to one side and asked him to stay at the woman's house. 'There,' said he, 'show her my card.' The rich uncle thought he might help the family a little.

Mrs Bell and both daughters were in the sitting room when Aaron Dunn was brought in, covered with snow. He told his story in a rough, shaky voice; his teeth were shaking with cold. And he gave the card, almost wishing that he had gone to the big empty hotel, as the welcome here was not very warm at first.

Mrs Bell listened to him as he gave his message, and then she took the card and looked at it. Hetta, who was sitting on the side of the fireplace facing the door, went on quietly with her work. Susan gave one look round – her back was to the stranger – and then another; and then she moved her chair a little nearer to the wall, to give the young man room to come to the fire, if he wished. He did not come, but he looked at Susan Bell; and he thought that the old man in New York was right, and that the big hotel would be cold and dull. It was a pretty face to look on, that cold evening, as she turned it up from her sewing.

'Perhaps you don't wish to take visitors in the winter, madam?' said Aaron Dunn.

'We have never done so yet, sir,' said Mrs Bell gently. Could she let this young man into the house among her daughters?

'Mr Bell seemed to think that it would be suitable,' said Aaron.

If he had not mentioned Mr Bell, it would all have been finished. But the woman did not like to go against the rich uncle; and so she said, 'Perhaps it may, sir.'

'I think it will,' said Aaron. And then he settled the weekly number of dollars – with very little difficulty, because he had seen Susan's face again – and went for his bag.

So Aaron Dunn entered Mrs Bell's house; but she was a little anxious that night. What kind of man was he? But then what if he was a strong honest man with a clever eye and hand, a ready brain, a broad back, and a warm heart? In need of a wife, perhaps; a man that could earn his own bread and another's bread. Would that not be a good sort of guest? Such a question as that did pass across the mother's sleepless mind. But he might be a worse kind of man. The worse kind was more common.

'I am surprised that Mother agreed to take him,' said Hetta, when the girls were alone together.

'And why shouldn't she?' said Susan. 'It will help us.'

'Yes, it will help us a little,' said Hetta. 'But we have done very well so far without winter guests.'

'But Uncle Bell said she must take him.'

'What is Uncle Bell to us?' said Hetta, who had a courage of her own. And she began to wonder whether Aaron Dunn would join in her religious work. And whether Phineas Beckard would be glad or not.

'He is a very well-behaved young man,' said Susan, 'and he draws beautifully. Did you see what he brought with him?'

'He draws very well, perhaps,' said Hetta, who thought this no proof of good behaviour. She had some fear for her sister.

Aaron Dunne's work – the beginning of his work – lay at some distance from the Springs, and he left every morning with a lot of workmen by an early train – almost before daylight. And every morning, although the mornings were cold and wintry, Hetta got him his breakfast with her own hands. She took his dollars, so that he was not completely left in the power of Kate O'Brien.

In the evening, leaving his work when it was dark, Aaron

57

returned, and then the evening was spent together. The women would make the tea, cut the bread and butter, and then sew; while Aaron Dunn, when the cups were taken away, would go to his plans and drawings.

On Sundays they were more together; but even on this day there was cause for separation, since they went to different churches. But in the afternoon they were all at home; and then Phineas Beckard came in to tea, and he and Aaron talked about religion. They disagreed a good deal, but the minister told the women that Aaron had good ideas in him.

Things went on in this way for more than a month. Aaron had told himself again and again that that face was sweet to look at, and had promised himself certain pleasures in talking and perhaps walking with the owner of it. But he had not yet succeeded in the walkings, or even the talkings. The truth was that Dunn was rather afraid of women.

And then he felt angry with himself because he had done nothing; and as he lay in his bed he decided that he would be a little braver. He had no idea of making love to Susan Bell; of course not. But why should he not amuse himself by talking to a pretty girl when she sat so near him, evening after evening?

'What a very quiet young man he is,' said Susan to her sister.

'He has his bread to earn, and so he works hard,' said Hetta. 'Probably he has his amusement when he is in the city.'

They all had their settled places in the sitting room. Hetta sat on one side of the fire, close to the table. There she was always busy; she must have made every dress worn in the house. Sometimes, once a week perhaps, Phineas Beckard came in, and then a place was made for him between Hetta's usual seat and the table. On the other side, close also to the table, sat the mother, busy, but not as busy as her daughter. Between Mrs Bell and the wall Susan would sit, doing a little work an talking sometimes to her mother. Opposite them all, at the other side of the table, far away from the fire, Aaron Dunn sat with his plans and drawings in front of him.

'Do you know a good bridge when you see it, madam?' said Aaron the evening after he had made his decision. This was how he began his lovemaking.

'Bridge?' cried Mrs Bell; 'oh, no, sir.' But she put out her hand to take the little drawing which Aaron handed to her.

'Because that's one I've planned for one part of the railway line. I think Miss Susan knows something about bridges.'

'I don't think so,' said Susan; 'only that they shouldn't fall down when the cold weather comes.'

'Ha, ha, ha! Quite right.'

'Oh, how pretty!' said the woman, and then Susan of course jumped up to look over her mother's shoulder.

The clever man! He had drawn and coloured a beautiful little picture of a bridge.

'Well, that is a pretty bridge,' said Susan. 'Isn't it, Hetta?'

'I don't know anything about bridges,' said Hetta. The trick was quite clear to her clever eyes. But Mrs Bell and Susan had soon moved their chairs round the table and were looking at Aaron's drawings.

'But he may be a bad man,' thought the poor mother, as she was kneeling down to say her prayers that night.

That evening Aaron had certainly made a start. Before bedtime he was teaching Susan how to use his drawing instruments. Susan liked it and had an enjoyable time that evening. It is dull to go on week after week, and month after month, talking only to one's mother and one's sister. Susan did not think of Aaron as a possible lover at all. But young ladies do like the conversations of young gentlemen.

Susan was happy when she went to bed; but Hetta was frightened at the trick.

'Oh, Hetta, you ought to have looked at those drawings. He is so clever!' said Susan.

'I don't think they would have done me much good,' replied Hetta.

'Good! They do me more good than going to church; except on Sunday, of course.' This was a bad-tempered attack on Hetta and Hetta's admirer, Phineas.

'I'm sure he's bad,' thought Hetta as she went to bed.

'What a very clever young man he is!' thought Susan to herself as she pulled the warm bedclothes round her shoulders and ears.

'Well, that was certainly better,' thought Aaron, as he did the same.

In the next two weeks Aaron sometimes read poetry to the others in the evenings. 'He reads much better than Mr Beckard,' Susan said one night. 'Of course, you're a good judge,' had been Hetta's reply. 'I mean that *I* like it better,' said Susan.

And then there was a great deal of talking. The mother herself talked freely and enjoyed it. And Beckard came there more often and talked a lot. There grew up a sort of friendship between the young men.

It was at the end of the second month when Aaron took another step – a dangerous step. In the evenings he still went on with his drawing for an hour or two; but for three or four evenings he did not ask anyone to look at what he was doing. One Friday he sat over his work until late, without any reading or talking at all; so late that at last Mrs Bell said, 'If you're going to sit much longer, Mr Dunn . . .'

'I've finished now,' said Aaron; and he looked carefully at the paper on which he had put his colours. 'I've finished now.' He paused for a moment, but then he carried the paper up to his bedroom with the rest. It was clear that it was intended as a present for Susan Bell.

The question which Aaron asked himself that night was this: should he offer the drawing to Susan in the presence of her mother and sister, or on some other occasion when they might be alone together? They had never been alone together yet, but Aaron thought they might be.

But he did not want to make it seem important. His first intention had been to throw the drawing carelessly across the table when it was completed, and to treat it as nothing. But he had finished it with more care than he had at first intended, and then he had paused when he had finished it. It was too late now to be careless about it.

On the Saturday evening when he came down from his room, Mr Beckard was there, and there was no opportunity that night. On the Sunday he went to church and walked with the family. This pleased Mrs Bell; but Sunday was not a suitable day for the picture.

On Monday the matter had become important to him. Things always do when they are delayed. Before tea that evening, when he came down, only Mrs Bell and Susan were in the room. He knew Hetta was his enemy, and therefore he decided to take this opportunity.

'Miss Susan,' he said slowly, his face a fiery red. 'I have done a little drawing which I want you to accept.'

'Oh! I'm not sure,' said Susan, who had seen the red face.

Mrs Bell had seen it too, and pressed her lips together and looked serious. If he had not paused, and if he had not gone red in the face, she might have thought it quite unimportant.

Aaron saw immediately that his little gift would not be accepted easily. But he picked it out of his other papers and brought it to Susan. He tried to hand it to her carelessly, but I cannot say that he succeeded.

It was a very pretty coloured drawing of the same bridge, but with more details. In Susan's eyes it was a work of high art. She had seen few pictures, and her liking for the artist no doubt added to her admiration. But the more she admired it and wished for it, the stronger was her feeling that she ought not to take it.

Poor Susan! She stood for a minute looking at the drawing, but she said nothing; not even a word of praise. She felt that she was red in the face, and impolite to their guest; but her mother was looking at her and she did not know how to behave.

Mrs Bell put out her hand for the drawing, trying to think how to refuse the present politely. She took a moment to look at it.

'Oh, dear, Mr Dunn, it is very pretty; quite a beautiful picture. I cannot let Susan take that from you. You must keep it for some of your own special friends.'

'But I did it for her,' said Aaron.

Susan looked down at the ground, half pleased with the words. The drawing would look pretty in a small frame over her dressing table. But the matter was now in her mother's hands.

'I am afraid it is too valuable, sir, for Susan to accept.'

'It is not valuable at all,' said Aaron, refusing to take it back from the woman's hand.

'Oh, I am quite sure it is. It is worth ten dollars at least – or twenty,' said poor Mrs Bell. The picture now lay on the tablecloth.

'It is not worth ten cents,' said Aaron. 'But as we had been talking about the bridge, I thought Miss Susan would accept it.'

'Accept what?' said Hetta, who had just come in. And then her eyes fell on the drawing and she picked it up.

'It is beautifully done,' said Mrs Bell gently. 'I am telling Mr Dunn that we can't take a present of anything so valuable.'

'Oh, no,' said Hetta. 'It wouldn't be right.'

It was a cold evening in March, and the fire was burning brightly. Aaron Dunn took up the drawing quietly – very quietly – and, rolling it up, put it between the burning pieces of wood. It was the work of four evenings, and the best picture he had ever done.

Susan, when she saw what he had done, burst into tears. Her mother could easily have done the same, but she was able to control herself and only cried, 'Oh, Mr Dunn!'

'If Mr Dunn wants to burn his own picture, he certainly has a right to do so,' said Hetta.

Aaron immediately felt ashamed of what he had done; and he also could have cried if he had not been a man. He walked away to one of the windows and looked out at the night. The stars were bright, and he thought that he would like to be walking fast by himself along the railway towards Balston. There he stood, perhaps for three minutes. He thought it would be proper to give Susan time to stop her tears.

'Will you please come to your tea, sir?' said Mrs Bell.

He turned round to do so, and found that Susan was gone. She could not stop her tears in three minutes. And the drawing had been so beautiful! It had been done especially for her too! And there had been something – she did not know what – in his eyes as he had said so. She had watched him closely during those four evenings' work; it was something very particular, she was sure, and she had learned that all the careful work had been for her. Now all that work was destroyed. How was it possible that she should not cry for more than three minutes?

The others had their meal in perfect silence, and when it was over the two women sat down to their work. Aaron had a book which he pretended to read, but instead of reading he was thinking that he had behaved badly. He was ashamed of what he had done, and he thought that Susan would hate him. He began to find at the same time that he by no means hated her.

At last Hetta got up and left the room. She knew that her sister was sitting alone in the cold. Susan had not been at fault and therefore Hetta went up to comfort her.

'Mrs Bell,' said Aaron as soon as the door was closed, 'I beg your pardon for what I did just now.'

'Oh, sir, I'm so sorry that the picture is burnt,' said poor Mrs Bell.

'The picture does not matter at all,' said Aaron. 'But I see that I have upset you all – and I am afraid I have made Miss Susan unhappy.'

'She was sorry because your picture was burnt,' said Mrs Bell.

'Oh, I can do 20 more of the same if anybody wants them,' said Aaron. 'If I do another like it, will you let her take it, Mrs Bell? Just to show that you have forgiven me.'

'But it mustn't have any meaning, sir,' was the woman's weak answer, when she had considered the question for a moment.

'No, no, of course not,' said Aaron joyfully, and his face became happy. 'And I do beg your pardon for burning it; and the young ladies' pardon too.' And then he rapidly got out his pencils, and set himself to work on another bridge. The woman, thinking of many things in her heart, began sewing a handkerchief.

In about an hour the two girls came back to the room and took their usual places silently. Aaron hardly looked up, but went on with his drawing. This bridge would be a better bridge than the other. He knew that it would be accepted. Of course it must mean nothing. So he said nothing to anybody.

When they went off to bed, the two girls went into their mother's room. 'Oh, Mother, I hope he is not very angry,' said Susan.

'Angry!' said Hetta. 'If anybody ought to be angry, it should be Mother. He ought to have known that Susan could not accept it. He should never have offered it.'

'But he's doing another,' said Mrs Bell.

'Not for her,' said Hetta.

'Yes, he is,' said Mrs Bell, 'and I have promised that she will take it.' As she heard this, Susan's eyes filled with tears. The meaning was almost more than she could bear.

'Oh, Mother!' said Hetta.

'But I particularly said that it must mean nothing.'

'Oh, Mother, that makes it worse.'

Susan wondered why Hetta wanted to get involved in this way. Had Susan said anything when Mr Beckard gave Hetta something? Had she not smiled and looked pleased, and kissed her sister, and declared that Phineas Beckard was a nice, dear man? Why was Hetta being so cruel?

'I don't understand that, my dear,' said the mother. Hetta refused to explain before her sister, and they all went to bed.

On the Thursday evening the drawing was finished. Not a word had been said about it in Aaron's presence, and he had gone on working in silence. 'There,' said he, late on Thursday evening, 'I don't think that it will be any better if I go on for another hour. There, Miss Susan; there's another bridge. I hope that it will neither burst with the cold nor be destroyed by fire,' and he passed it across the table.

Susan's face was red when she smiled and picked it up. 'Oh, it is beautiful,' she said. 'Isn't it beautifully done, Mother?' and then all three got up to look at it, and all admitted that it was excellently done.

'And I am sure we thank you very much,' said Susan after a pause.

'Oh, it's nothing,' said he, not quite liking the word 'we'.

On the following day he returned from his work to Saratoga at about midday. He had never done this before, and therefore no one expected that he would be seen in the house before the evening. Susan was there alone in charge of the house.

He walked in and opened the sitting room door. There she sat, with her work forgotten on the table behind her, and the picture, Aaron's drawing, on her knees. She was looking at it closely as he entered, thinking in her young heart that it possessed all the beauties that a picture could possess.

'Oh, Mr Dunn,' she said, getting up and holding the picture behind her dress.

'Miss Susan, I have come here to tell your mother that I must

65

start for New York this afternoon and be there for six weeks, or perhaps longer.'

'Mother is out,' said she; 'I'm so sorry.'

'Is she?' said Aaron.

'And Hetta too. Dear me! And you will want dinner. I'll go and see about it.'

Aaron began to swear that he could not possibly eat any dinner. He had had one dinner, and he was going to have another – anything to keep her from going.

'But you must have something, Mr Dunn,' and she walked towards the door.

But he put his back to it. 'Miss Susan,' said he, 'I've been here for nearly two months.'

'Yes, sir, I believe you have,' she replied, shaking in her shoes and not knowing which way to look.

'And I hope we have been good friends.'

'Yes, sir,' said Susan, hardly knowing what she was saying.

'I'm going away now, and it will be a long time before I'm back.'

'Will it, sir?'

'Six weeks, Miss Susan!' And there he paused, looking into her eyes, to see what he could read there. She leant against the table, pulling to pieces a handkerchief which she held in her hand; but her eyes were turned to the ground, and he could hardly see them.

'Miss Susan,' he continued, 'this is as good a time to speak as any other.' He too was looking towards the ground, and clearly did not know what to do with his hands. 'The truth is just this. I – I love you dearly, with all my heart. I never saw anyone I thought so beautiful, so nice, so good; and what's more, I never shall. I'm not very good at saying things like this, I know; but I couldn't go away from Saratoga for six weeks and not tell you.' And then he stopped. He did not ask for any love in return. He simply declared his feelings, leaning against the door.

66

Susan had not the slightest idea of the way in which she ought to reply to such words. She had never had a lover before; nor had she thought of Aaron exactly as a lover, though it is true she had been feeling something very like love for him. Now, at this moment, she thought that he was the best possible man, though his shoes were covered with railway mud, and his clothes were rough. He was a fine, well-built, honest man, whose eye was brave but gentle. Love him! Of course she loved him.

But what must she say? Not the whole truth; she well knew that. What would her mother and Hetta say if she told the truth? Hetta, she knew, would be against such a lover, and she had hardly more hope of her mother's agreement. She never asked herself why they disliked Aaron as a lover for her. There are many nice things that seem to be wrong only because they are nice. Perhaps Susan thought of a lover as one of them. 'Oh, Mr Dunn, you shouldn't.' That in fact was all that she could say.

'Shouldn't I?' said he. 'Well, perhaps not; but there's the truth, and no harm ever comes of that. Perhaps it's better for me not to ask for an answer now, but I thought it better that you should know it all. And remember this – I only care for one thing now in the world, and that is for your love.' And then he paused, hoping that perhaps he might get some sort of an answer, some idea of her heart's feelings towards him.

But Susan had immediately decided to agree when he suggested that an immediate reply was not necessary. To say that she loved him was of course impossible, and to say that she did not was equally so. She therefore decided to be silent.

He tried hard to read what might be written on her down-turned face, but he was not good at such reading. 'Well, I'll go and get my things ready now,' he said, and then turned to open the door.

'Mother will come home before you are gone, I suppose,' said Susan.

'I have only got 20 minutes,' said he, looking at his watch. 'But, Susan, tell her what I have said to you. Goodbye.' And he put out his hand. He knew he would see her again, but this had been his plan to get her hand into his.

'Goodbye, Mr Dunn,' and she gave him her hand.

He held it tight for a moment, so that she could not pull it away. 'Will you tell your mother?' he asked.

'Yes,' she answered, quite in a whisper. 'I think it's better to tell her.' He pressed her hand again and got it to his lips.

'Mr Dunn, don't,' she said. But he did kiss it. 'God keep you, my own dearest, dearest girl! I'll just open the door as I come down. Perhaps Mrs Bell will be here.'

But Mrs Bell did not come in. Susan, when left alone, sat down and tried to think. But she could not think; she could only love. She thought of the young god whose heavy steps could be heard upstairs as he walked around collecting things and putting them into his bag.

And then, just when he had finished, she remembered that he must be hungry. She ran to the kitchen, but she was too late. Before she could even reach the bread he came down the stairs.

'Miss Susan,' he said, 'don't get anything for me; I'm going now.'

'Oh, Mr Dunn, I am sorry. You'll be hungry on your journey,' and she came out to him in the passage.

'I shall want nothing on the journey, dearest, if you'll say one kind word to me.'

Again her eyes fell to the ground. 'What do you want me to say, Mr Dunn?'

'Say, God keep you, Aaron.'

'God keep you, Aaron,' said she; but she was sure that she had not stated her love. He thought differently, though, and went to New York with a happy heart.

Things happened rather quickly in the next two weeks. Susan

68

decided to tell her mother, but not Hetta. She spoke to her mother that afternoon.

'And what did you say to him, Susan?'

'Nothing, Mother; not a word. He told me he didn't want it.' She forgot how she had used his first name in asking God to keep him.

'Oh dear!' said her mother.

'Was it very wrong?' asked Susan.

'But what do you think yourself, my child?' asked Mrs Bell after a time. 'What are your own feelings?'

Mrs Bell was sitting on a chair, and Susan was standing opposite her. She made no answer but, moving from her place, she threw herself into her mother's arms and hid her face on her mother's shoulder. It was easy enough to guess what her feelings were.

'But, my dear,' said her mother, 'you must not think that you are promised in marriage.'

'No,' said Susan sorrowfully.

'Young men say these things to amuse themselves.'

'Oh, Mother, he is not like that.'

The daughter managed to get a promise that Hetta should not be told just at present. Mrs Bell calculated that she had six weeks before her; Mr Beckard had not asked Hetta to marry him yet, but there was reason to think that he would do so before those six weeks were over, and then she would be able to ask him for advice.

Mr Beckard spoke out at the end of six days, and Hetta immediately accepted him. 'I hope you'll love him,' she said to Susan.

'Oh, I will, I will,' said Susan; and she nearly told her secret. But Hetta was thinking of her own affairs.

It was then arranged that Hetta should go and spend a week with Mr Beckard's parents. Old Mr Beckard was a farmer living near Utah, and it was thought a good idea that Hetta should know her future husband's family. So she went for a week, and Mr Beckard went with her. 'He will be back in plenty of time for me to speak to him before Aaron Dunn's six weeks are over,' said Mrs Bell to herself.

But things did not go exactly as she had expected. On the morning after the two went away, there came a letter from Aaron saying that he would be at Saratoga that evening. The railway people had ordered him to come back for some days' special work; then he would go away again, and not come back to Saratoga until June.

'Oh dear, oh dear!' said Mrs Bell to herself, thinking that she had no one to advise her. Why had she let Mr Beckard go without telling him? Then she told Susan, and Susan spent the day trembling. Perhaps, thought Mrs Bell, he will say nothing about it. But then would it not be her duty to say something? Poor mother! She trembled nearly as much as Susan.

It was dark when the knock came at the door. The tea things were laid, and the tea cake was ready; since it would be necessary in any case to give Mr Dunn his tea. Susan, when she heard the knock, rushed upstairs. Kate O'Brien opened the door, and welcomed her old friend.

'How are the ladies?' asked Aaron, trying to learn something from the servant's face and voice.

'Miss Hetta and Mr Beckard have gone off to Utah, just like man and wife.'

'Oh, really; I'm very glad,' said Aaron – and so he was; very glad to have Hetta away. And then he went to the sitting room, doubting much and hoping much.

Mrs Bell rose from her chair, and tried to look serious. Aaron saw that Susan was not in the room. He walked straight up to the woman and offered her his hand, which she took. Perhaps Susan had not told; so he said nothing.

But the subject was too important to the mother to allow her to be silent when the young man stood before her. 'Oh, Mr Dunn,' she said, 'what is this that you have been saying to Susan?'

'I have asked her to be my wife,' said he, standing up straight and looking her full in the face. Mrs Bell's heart was almost as soft as her daughter's; but at the time she said only 'Oh dear, oh dear!'

'May I not call you Mother?' said he, taking both her hands in his.

'Oh dear, oh dear; but will you be good to her? Oh, Aaron Dunn, if you deceive my child!'

In another quarter of an hour, Susan was kneeling at her mother's knee with tears in her eyes, and Aaron was holding one of her mother's hands.

'You are my mother too, now,' said he. What would Hetta and Mr Beckard say when they came back?

There were four or five days left before they would come back; four or five days during which Susan might be happy, Aaron glad, and Mrs Bell nervous. But it was really only the evenings that were left of the days. Every morning Susan got up to give Aaron his breakfast, but Mrs Bell got up too. After that Aaron was always out until seven or eight in the evening, when he came home for his tea. Then came the hour or two of lovers' meeting.

But they were very dull, those hours. The mother was still afraid that she was wrong, and although she wanted her daughter to be happy, she feared to be too sure. Not a word had been said about money matters, not a word of Aaron Dunn's relations. So she did not leave the young people by themselves, but waited patiently for her wise advisers to come back.

And Susan hardly knew how to behave with Aaron. She felt that she was very happy; but perhaps she was happiest when she was thinking about him through the long day, arranging little things for his comfort, and waiting for the evening. And as he sat

71

there in the sitting room she could be happy too, if she were only allowed to sit still and look at him.

But he wanted to hear her speak, and perhaps thought he had the right to sit by her and hold her hand. No such rights were given to him. If they had been alone together, walking side by side as lovers ought to walk, she could have spoken to him. But though there was much love between Aaron and Susan, they were not close friends yet. And her mother's presence prevented easy conversation. Aaron was very fond of Mrs Bell, but he did sometimes wish that her housework would take her out of the sitting room for a few happy minutes.

Once for a moment he did find his love alone, when he returned to the house. 'My own Susan, do you love me? Do say so to me once.' And he managed to put his arm round her. 'Yes,' she whispered; but then she slipped away from him. And when she reached her room she felt that she really did love him deeply with a love that filled her whole life. Why could she not have told him something of all this?

And so the few days of his second stay at Saratoga passed away not very satisfactorily. It was arranged that he should return to New York on Saturday night, leaving Saratoga on that evening. And as Hetta and Mr Beckard were arriving back to dinner on that day, Mrs Bell would have an opportunity of telling her wonderful news. It might be a good thing for Mr Beckard to see Aaron before he left.

They came in time for dinner, and talked about all their arrangements. After dinner Susan disappeared immediately, and her mother told Hetta.

'Asked her to marry him!' said Hetta, who perhaps thought that one marriage in a family was enough at one time.

'Yes, my dear – and he did it, I must say, in a very honourable way, telling her not to make any answer until she had spoken to me. That was very nice; was it not, Phineas?'

'And what has been said to him since then?' asked Phineas.

'Nothing definite,' said Mrs Bell. 'I know nothing about his financial affairs.'

'He is a man who will always earn his bread,' said Mr Beckard; and Mrs Bell blessed him in her heart for saying it.

'But has he been encouraged?' asked Hetta.

'Well, yes, he has,' said her mother.

'Then Susan, I suppose, likes him?' asked Phineas.

'Well, yes, she does,' said the woman.

It was decided that Phineas should have a talk with Aaron about his worldly position, and decide whether Aaron could be accepted as a lover.

When Beckard spoke to Aaron, the latter declared that he had nothing except what he made as an engineer. He said that he was well paid just then, but would have to look for other work at the end of the summer.

'Then you can hardly marry at present,' said the minister.

'Perhaps not quite immediately. In three or four months, perhaps.'

But Mr Beckard shook his head.

The afternoon at Mrs Bell's house was sad. The decision was as follows. There could be no promise, and of course no letters. Aaron would be told that it would be better for him to stay somewhere else when he returned; but that he would be allowed to visit Mrs Bell's house. If he got better and more permanent work, of course, and if Susan still felt the same . . . This was what Mrs Bell and Hetta told Susan. She sat still and cried when she heard it, but she was not surprised. She had always felt that Hetta would be against her.

'Am I not allowed to see him then?' she said through her tears.

Hetta thought she had better not. Mrs Bell thought perhaps she could. Phineas decided that they could shake hands when all the others were present. There should be no lovers' goodbye. Poor Susan!

Susan was gentle and womanly. But Aaron was not very gentle and he was a man. When Mr Beckard told him of the decision, there came over his face the look which he had worn when he burned the picture. He said that Mrs Bell had encouraged him, and he did not understand why other people should now come and change things.

'It was not a promise,' said Mrs Bell sorrowfully.

He said that he was ready and able to work and knew his profession and asked what young man of his age had done better than he had.

Then Mr Beckard spoke out, very wisely no doubt, but for too long a time. Sons and daughters, as well as fathers and mothers, will know what he said; so I need not repeat the words. I cannot say that Aaron listened with much attention.

'Mrs Bell,' said Aaron. 'I think of myself as promised to Susan. And I think of Susan as promised to me. And I think she wishes to be.'

'But, Aaron, you won't try to see her or write to her in secret, will you?'

'When I try to see her, I'll come and knock at this door; and if I write to her, I'll write to the full address by the post. I never did and never will do anything in secret.'

'I know you're good and honest,' said the woman, with her handkerchief to her eyes.

'Then why do you separate us?' he asked, almost roughly. 'I suppose I may see her before I go? It's nearly time now.'

And then Susan was called for. She came with Hetta, and her eyes were red with crying.

'Goodbye, Susan,' said Aaron, and he walked up to her quite openly; his temper was hot. She took his hand and he held it until he had finished speaking. 'Remember this: I think of you as my promised wife.'

'Goodbye, Aaron,' she said through her tears.

'Goodbye, and God bless you, my dearest!' And then, without saying a word to anyone else, he turned his back on them and left.

There had been something very sweet to the poor girl in her lover's last words, but he seemed to feel nothing but anger for the others. She knew that she could never, never stop loving him better than all the world. She would wait patiently, and then, if he did not come back, she would die.

In another month Hetta became Mrs Beckard. The summer came and the house was full of guests. Susan was busy. Aaron did not come back to Saratoga: during the whole long summer they heard not a word from him. And then the cold winter months came, and the guests left. It was a sad winter.

They learned nothing of Aaron Dunn until about January; and then they heard that he was doing well. He had work on a railway, was highly paid, and was much respected. But still he neither came nor wrote!

After that Mrs Bell thought it her duty to teach her daughter that she would see Aaron Dunn no more. He had the right to leave her. He had been driven from the house when he was poor, and they had no right to expect that he would return. 'Men do amuse themselves in that way,' said the woman.

'He is not like that,' the daughter replied.

And so, through the long winter months, Susan became paler and paler, and thinner and thinner.

Hetta tried to comfort her sister with religion; but it was of little use. She thought that Susan was wrong to grow thin and pale through love of Aaron; so Susan in those days found no comfort in her sister. But her mother's soft pity and love did make her suffering easy to bear.

'He will never come again,' said Susan one day.

'My dear,' said her mother, pressing her child closely to her side. 'I do not think he will.'

Then the hot tears ran down Susan's face. 'Was I wrong to love him?' she asked.

'No, my child; you were no wrong at all.'

The next morning Susan did not get up. She was not ill, she said, but very tired. Her mother's heart was full of sorrow for her child. Oh, why had she driven away the love of an honest man?

On the next morning Susan again did not get up – so she did not hear the step of the postman, who brought a letter to the door. The letter which he brought was as follows:

My dear Mrs Bell,

I have now got a permanent post on the railway line, and the salary is enough for myself and a wife. That is what I think, and I hope you will too. I shall be at Saratoga tomorrow evening, and I hope neither Susan nor you will refuse to receive me.

Yours,

AARON DUNN.

It was very short, and did not contain one word of love. But it made the woman's heart jump for joy. She was afraid that Aaron was angry, because the letter was so short; but surely he had only one aim in coming.

How could she tell Susan? She ran upstairs almost breathless with speed; but then she stopped: too much joy was as dangerous as too much sorrow; she must think for a time.

After breakfast she went into Susan's room.

'Susan dear,' she said, and smiled, 'you'll be able to get up this morning, perhaps?'

'Yes, Mother.'

'I don't mean at this moment, my love. I want to sit with you for a short time.'

'Dearest Mother,' said Susan.

'Ah! there's someone dearer than I am,' and Mrs Bell smiled sweetly.

Susan raised herself quickly in the bed. 'Mother, what is it? You've something to tell. Oh Mother! You've got a letter. Is he coming?' She sat up with eager eyes.

'Yes, dear. I have got a letter.'

'Is he – is he coming?'

How the mother answered I can hardly tell; but she did answer. It was hard to say who was the happier.

Aaron was coming that evening. 'Oh, Mother, let me get up.'

But Mrs Bell said no, not yet. Her dear daughter was pale and thin. Suppose he came and saw her and, finding her beauty gone, disappeared again and looked for a wife somewhere else. So Susan lay in bed, sleeping sometimes and fearing as she woke that it was a dream. She often looked at the drawing, which she kept on the bed, and tried to think what she should say to him.

'Mother,' she said when Mrs Bell once went up to her, 'you won't tell Hetta and Phineas, will you?' Mrs Bell agreed.

When Susan got up, she asked her mother what to wear. 'If he loves you,' said her mother, 'he will hardly see what you are wearing.' But she was careful to brush her daughter's hair.

How Susan's heart beat – how both their hearts beat as the hands of the clock came round to seven! And then, exactly at seven, that same sharp knock came. 'Oh, Mother, I must go upstairs,' cried Susan, jumping from her chair.

'No, dear.'

'I will, Mother.'

'No, dear; you have not time.' And then Aaron Dunn was in the room.

She had thought a lot about what to say to him; but it mattered very little. Aaron Dunn came into the room, and in one second she found herself in the centre of a storm, and his arms were the storm that surrounded her on every side.

'My own, my dearest girl,' he said again and again.

'Aaron, dear Aaron,' she whispered. She knew that she had her lover there safe, whatever Mr and Mrs Beckard might say. She was quite happy.

'Dear Aaron, I am so glad that you have come,' said Mrs Bell, as she went upstairs with him to show him his room.

'Dear, dear Mother,' he said.

On the next day Hetta and Phineas came and talked about the marriage with Mrs Bell. Hetta at first was not quite certain. 'Shouldn't we find out if the post is really permanent?' she said.

'I won't ask at all,' said Mrs Bell in a decisive voice that made Hetta and Phineas jump. 'I shall not separate them now.'

'He is a good man,' said Phineas. 'And I hope she will make him a good, steady wife.' And so the matter was settled.

During this time Susan and Aaron were walking along the road; and they had also settled the matter quite satisfactorily.

Lord Mountdrago   *W. Somerset Maugham*

Doctor Audlin looked at the clock on his desk. It was twenty minutes to six. He was surprised that Lord Mountdrago was late, since he had always been on time for previous appointments. Lord Mountdrago's appointment today was for half past five.

There was in Dr Audlin's appearance nothing to attract attention. He was tall and thin, with narrow shoulders; he was a little bent; his hair was thin and grey; his long pale face was deeply lined. He was not more than fifty, but he looked older. His eyes, pale blue and rather large, were tired. When you had been with him for a time, you noticed that they moved very little; they remained fixed on your face, but they were so empty of expression that this caused no discomfort. They gave no idea of his thoughts, nor changed with the words he spoke. His hands were rather large, with long fingers; they were soft, but firm. You could never have described what Dr Audlin wore unless you looked specifically. His clothes were dark. His tie was black. His dress made his pale face paler.

Dr Audlin was a psychoanalyst who had entered the profession by accident. When the war started he had not been working long and was gaining experience at different hospitals; he offered his services, and after a time was sent out to France. It was then that he discovered his strange qualities. He could stop certain pains by the touch of his firm hands, and by talking to men who were suffering from sleeplessness, he could often cause them to sleep. He spoke slowly. His voice had no particular quality, and its sound did not change with the words he used, but it was musical and soft. He told the men that they must rest, that they mustn't worry, that they must sleep; and the rest seemed to slip into their tired bones; calmness pushed their anxieties away, and sleep fell on their tired eyelids like the light rain of spring on the earth. Dr Audlin found that by speaking to men in his low voice, by looking at them with his pale, quiet eyes, by touching their tired heads with his long firm hands, he could calm them. Sometimes he performed cures that seemed like miracles. He brought back speech to a man who was unable to speak after being buried under the earth in an explosion; and he gave back the use of his legs to a man who could not move after his plane was shot down. He could not understand his powers, but the results of his work were clear to everyone, and he had to admit to himself that he had some strange quality that allowed him to do things for which he could offer no explanation.

When the war was over he went to Vienna and studied there, and afterwards to Zurich; and then he settled in London to practise the art which he had so strangely learnt. He had been practising now for fifteen years and was well known. People told one another of the astonishing things he had done, and through his charges were high, many came to him for his advice. He knew that he had done a great deal of good in the world; he had brought back health and happiness to many. But at the back of his mind he was never quite sure how he had done so.

He did not like using a power which he could not understand, and he thought it was dishonest to make money from patients who believed in him when he had no belief in himself. He was rich enough now to live without working, and the work made him very tired. He had seen a lot of human nature during his 15 years in Wimpole Street. The stories that had been told to him, sometimes easily, sometimes with shame, with anger, had stopped surprising him long ago. Nothing could shock him any more. He knew by now that men were liars, that they were proud; he knew far worse than that about them, but he also knew that it was not his duty to judge. But year after year these terrible truths told to him made his face a little greyer, its lines a little more marked and his pale eyes more tired. He rarely laughed, but sometimes when he read a book he smiled. Did the writers really think men and women were like that? Real people had much darker, more complicated souls.

It was a quarter to six. Dr Audlin could remember no case which was stranger than that of Lord Mountdrago. For one thing it was strange because Lord Mountdrago was a successful and famous man. He had been appointed Foreign Minister when still under forty years of age, and it was generally agreed that he was the cleverest man in his party. There was nothing to prevent Lord Mountdrago from continuing as Foreign Minister in later governments.

Lord Mountdrago had many good qualities. He was intelligent and worked hard. He had travelled widely and spoke several languages well. He knew a great deal about other countries. He had courage and determination. He was a good speaker. He was a tall, good-looking man, though perhaps rather heavy. At the age of twenty-four he had married a girl of eighteen whose father was a lord and whose American mother was very rich, so that he had a good position and wealth. He also had two sons. He had, in fact, much of what was necessary to make him a popular and successful man. But unfortunately he also had many faults.

He was very proud of his social position. For 300 years his family had held the title of Lord Mountdrago and had married into the oldest families of England. But he still never missed an opportunity of telling others about it. He had beautiful manners when he wanted to show them, but he did this only with people whom he considered his equals. He was rude to his servants and his secretaries. The lower officials in the government offices feared and hated him. He knew that he was a great deal cleverer than most of the people he worked with, and never missed an opportunity of telling them so. He had no patience with the weaknesses of human nature. He felt himself born to command

and was angry when people expected him to listen to their arguments or wished to hear the reasons for his decisions. He had many enemies to whom he showed no pity. He had no friends. He was unpopular with his party because he was so proud; but he loved his country so much and managed affairs so well that they had to accept his faults. It was possible to do this because sometimes he could be quite charming. He could be the best company in the world, and you could forget that he had insulted you the day before and was quite able to insult you again.

Lord Mountdrago had almost failed to become Dr Audlin's patient. A secretary had telephoned the doctor and told him that his lordship would be glad if the doctor would come to his house at ten o'clock on the following morning. Dr Audlin answered that he was unable to go to Lord Mountdrago's house, but would be pleased to see him in Wimpole Street on the day after that. The secretary took the message and telephoned again to say that Lord Mountdrago was determined to see Dr Audlin in his own house and the doctor could charge what he liked. Dr Audlin replied that he only saw people in his own room and explained that unless Lord Mountdrago was prepared to come to him, he could not give him his attention. In a quarter of an hour a short message was delivered to him that his lordship would come, not in two days' time but the next day, at five o'clock.

When Lord Mountdrago was announced, he did not come forward, but stood at the door and looked the doctor up and down. Dr Audlin could see that he was very angry. He saw a big, heavy man, with greying hair, a swollen face and a cold, proud expression. He had the look of an eighteenth-century French king.

'It seems that it is extremely difficult to see you, Dr Audlin. I'm a very busy man.'

'Won't you sit down?' said the doctor.

His face showed no sign that Lord Mountdrago's speech had

had any effect on him. Dr Audlin sat in his chair at the desk. Lord Mountdrago still stood and looked angrier.

'I think I should tell you that I am the Foreign Minister,' he said sharply.

'Won't you sit down?' the doctor repeated.

Lord Mountdrago made a movement which appeared to suggest that he was about to turn and leave the room; but if that was his intention, he seemed to change his mind. He sat down. Dr Audlin opened a large book and took up his pen. He wrote without looking at his patient.

'How old are you?'

'Forty-two.'

'Are you married?'

'Yes.'

'How long have you been married?'

'Eighteen years.'

'Have you any children?'

'I have two sons.'

Dr Audlin wrote down the facts as Lord Mountdrago answered. Then he leaned back in his chair and looked at him. He did not speak; he just looked, with pale blue eyes that did not move.

'Why have you come to see me?' he asked at last.

'I've heard about you. Lady Canute comes to see you, I believe. She tells me you've done a certain amount of good.'

Dr Audlin did not reply. His eyes remained fixed on the other's face, but they were so empty of expression that you might have thought he did not even see him.

'I can't perform miracles,' he said at last. Not a smile, but the shadow of a smile, passed over his eyes.

Lord Mountdrago spoke in a more friendly way. 'You have a good name. People seem to believe in you.'

'Why have you come to see me?' repeated Dr Audlin.

Now it was Lord Mountdrago's turn to be silent. It looked as though he found it hard to answer. Dr Audlin waited. At last Lord Mountdrago seemed to make an effort. He spoke.

'I'm in perfect health. I was examined by my own doctor just recently. He's Sir Augustus Fitzherbert. Perhaps you've heard of him. He tells me I'm as fit as a man of thirty. I work hard, but I'm never tired, and I enjoy my work. I smoke very little and do not drink much. I take enough exercise and I lead a regular life. I am a perfectly normal, healthy man. I quite expect you to think me childish in coming to see you.'

Dr Audlin saw that he must help him.

'I don't know if I can do anything for you. I'll try. You're unhappy?'

'My present work is important. The decisions that I have to make affect the country and even the peace of the world. It is necessary that my judgement should be good and my brain clear. I consider it my duty to rid myself of any cause of worry that may prevent this.'

Dr Audlin had never taken his eyes off him. He saw a great deal. He saw behind the man's pride an anxiety that he could not get rid of.

'I asked you to be good enough to come here because I know by experience that it's easier for someone to speak openly in a doctor's room than in his usual surroundings.'

It was clear that Lord Mountdrago, usually so quick and decided, at this moment did not know what to say. He smiled to show the doctor that he was relaxed, but his eyes showed his real feelings. He spoke again.

'The whole thing's so unimportant that I can hardly bring myself to trouble you with it. I'm afraid you'll just tell me not to be a fool and waste your valuable time.'

'Even things that seem unimportant may have their importance. They can be signs of deeper troubles. And my time is at your service.'

Dr Audlin's voice was low and serious. It was strangely calming. Lord Mountdrago at last made up his mind to speak openly.

'The fact is I've been having some dreams recently that have been bothering me. I know it's foolish to pay any attention to them, but — well, the honest truth is they've begun to have an effect on my nerves.'

'Can you describe any of them to me?'

'They're so foolish, I can hardly begin to tell them.'

'Never mind.'

'Well, the first I had was about a month ago. I dreamt that I was at a party at Connemara House. It was an official party. The King and Queen were going to be there. I went to take off my coat and there was a little man in the room called Owen Griffiths, who's a Welsh Member of Parliament, and to tell you the truth, I was surprised to see him. He's very common, and I said to myself, "Really, Lydia Connemara shouldn't have asked him to her house. Whom will she ask next?" I thought that he looked at me rather strangely, but I didn't take any notice of him; in fact I did not speak a word and I walked upstairs. I suppose you've never been there?'

'Never.'

'No, it's not the sort of house you would ever go to. It's in rather bad taste, but it's got a very fine stone staircase, and the Connemaras were at the top receiving their guests. Lady Connemara gave me a look of surprise when I shook hands with her, and began to laugh. I didn't pay much attention; she's a foolish woman and her manners are no better than those of her relatives. I must say the rooms at Connemara House are very grand. I walked through, shaking hands with a number of people. Then I saw the German minister talking with an Austrian lord. I particularly wanted to have a word with him, so I went up and held out my hand. As soon as he saw me he burst out laughing. I was deeply insulted. I looked him up and down, but he only laughed louder. I was about to speak to him rather sharply, when the room suddenly went quiet, and I realized that the King and Queen had come. Turning my back on him, I stepped forward, and then, quite suddenly, I noticed that I hadn't got any trousers on. I was wearing silk underclothes. It was not surprising that Lady Connemara and the German minister had laughed. I can't tell you how I felt at that moment. The shame! I awoke shaking. Oh, you don't know how glad I felt to find it was only a dream.'

'It's the kind of dream that's not so very uncommon,' said Dr Audlin.

'Perhaps not. But a strange thing happened the next day. I was in the House of Commons when Griffiths walked past me. He looked down at my legs and then he looked me in the face, and there was something in his eyes that made me feel he was laughing at me. A foolish thought came to me – he had been there the night before, and now he was enjoying the joke. But of course I knew that was impossible because it was only a dream. I gave him an icy look and he walked on. But he was laughing.'

Lord Mountdrago took his handkerchief out of his pocket and rubbed it over his hands. He was making no attempt now to hide his anxiety. Dr Audlin never took his eyes off him.

'Tell me another dream.'

'It was the next night. I dreamt that I was in the House of Commons. We were discussing foreign affairs and not only the country but the whole world was waiting for the discussion with serious interest. It was, in fact, a historic occasion. Of course the House was crowded. Representatives of foreign countries were there. I had to make the most important speech of the evening. I had prepared it carefully. A man like me has enemies. A lot of people are jealous because I have reached the position I have at an early age, and I was determined to speak well. I rose to my feet. When I began to speak, the silence was like the silence of the grave. Suddenly, though, I saw that hateful little devil on one of the seats opposite, Griffiths, the Welsh member; he put out his tongue at me ... I don't know if you've ever heard a song called "A Bicycle Made For Two". It was very popular many years ago. To show Griffiths my disgust for him I began to sing it. I sang the first part right through. There was a moment's surprise, and when I finished they cried 'Hear, hear,' from the opposition seats to express their approval. I put up my hand to silence them and sang the second part. The members listened to me in complete silence and I felt that the song wasn't being received very well. I was angry, because I have a good voice, and I was determined that they should be fair to me. When I started the third part the members began to laugh; in a moment the laughter spread. Everyone in the House shook; they cheered, they held their sides, they rolled on the seats. Everyone was helpless with laughter except the government ministers just behind me. They sat as if turned to stone. I gave them a look, and I suddenly understood the terrible thing that I had done. The whole world would laugh at me. I realized that I would have to leave my post in the government. I woke and realized that it was only a dream.'

Lord Mountdrago's proud manner had left him as he told this, and now, having finished, he was pale and trembling. But with an effort he regained his calm. He forced a laugh to his shaking lips.

'The whole thing was so crazy that I couldn't help being amused. I didn't give it another thought, and when I went into the House on the following afternoon I was feeling good. I sat in my place and read some papers that demanded my attention. For some reason I chanced to look up and I saw that Griffiths was speaking. I couldn't imagine that he had anything to say that was worth listening to, and I was about to return to my papers when he mentioned two lines from "A Bicycle Made For Two". I couldn't help looking at him, and I saw that his eyes were fixed on me and that there was a cruel smile on his lips. I didn't care. It was just strange that he'd included in his speech two lines from that terrible song that I'd sung in my dream. I began to read my papers again, but I found it difficult to think about them. Owen Griffiths had been in my first dream, the one at Connemara House, and I thought afterwards that he knew how foolish I had looked. Was it pure chance that he'd used those two lines from the song? I asked myself if it was possible that he was dreaming the same dreams as I was. But of course it wasn't, and I decided not to give it a second thought.'

There was a silence. Dr Audlin looked at Lord Mountdrago and Lord Mountdrago looked at Dr Audlin.

'Other people's dreams are very uninteresting. My wife used to dream occasionally and always told me her dreams the next day with every detail: It nearly drove me mad.'

Dr Audlin smiled faintly. 'I'm interested in your dreams.'

'I'll tell you one more dream that I had a few days later. I dreamt that I went into a bar in Limehouse. I've never been to Limehouse in my life and I don't think I've been in a public bar for a drink since I was at university, but I saw the street and the place I went into very clearly. I went into a room; there was a fireplace and a large leather chair on one side of it, and on the other a long seat. Near the door was a round table with two big chairs beside it. It was a Saturday night and the place was crowded. It was brightly lit, but the smoke was so thick that it made my eyes hurt. I was dressed like a working-class man, with a cap on my head and a handkerchief round my neck. It seemed to me that most of the people there were drunk. I thought it rather amusing. There was a radio and in front of the fireplace two women were doing a mad sort of dance. There was a little crowd round them, laughing and singing. I went to have a look, and a man said to me, "Have a drink, Bill?" There were glasses on the table full of dark beer. He gave me a glass and I drank it. One of the women who were dancing left the other and took hold of the glass. "What are you doing?" she said. "That's mine." "Oh, I'm sorry," I said. "This gentleman offered it to me." "All right," she said, "it doesn't matter. Come and have a dance with me." Before I could object, she had caught hold of me and we were dancing together. And then I found myself sitting in the leather chair and the woman and I were sharing a drink. I should tell you that women have never played any great part in my life. I've always been too busy to give much thought to that kind of thing. This woman was drunk; she wasn't pretty and she wasn't young. She filled me with disgust. Suddenly I heard a voice. "That's right, my friend, have a good time." I looked up and there was Owen Griffiths. I tried to jump out of the chair but that terrible woman didn't let me. "Don't pay any attention to him," she said. "Enjoy yourself," he said.

'I pushed the woman away and stood up and faced him. "I don't know you and I don't want to know you," I said. "I know *you*, all right," he said. There was a bottle standing on the table close to me. Without a word I seized it by the neck and hit him over the head with it as hard as I could. The blow was so violent that it woke me up.'

'A dream of that sort is easily understandable,' said Dr Audlin. 'It is the revenge which nature takes on people of good character.'

'The story's crazy. But again, it's what happened the next day that worries me. I wanted to look at a book in a hurry and I went into the parliamentary library. I got the book and began reading. I hadn't noticed when I sat down that Griffiths was sitting in a chair close to me. Another member came in and went up to him. "Hullo, Owen," he said to him, "you're looking ill today." "I've got a terrible headache," he answered. "I feel as if someone's hit me on the head with a bottle."'

Now Lord Mountdrago's face was grey with anxiety.

'I knew then that the idea which I had dismissed as foolish was true. I knew that Griffiths was dreaming my dreams and that he remembered them as well as I did.'

'It may also have been chance.'

'When he spoke, he wasn't speaking to his friend. He was speaking to me.'

'Can you explain why this same man should come into your dreams?'

'No, I can't.'

Dr Audlin's eyes had not left Lord Mountdrago's face, and he saw that he was lying. He had a pencil in his hand and he drew a line or two on a bit of paper. It often took a long time to make people tell the truth; but they knew that unless they told it he could do nothing for them.

'The dream you've just described happened just over three weeks ago. Have you had any since?'

'Every night.'

'And does this man Griffiths come into them all?'

'Yes.'

The doctor drew some more lines on the paper. He wanted the silence of the room to have its effect on Lord Mountdrago. Lord Mountdrago turned his head away from the other's serious eyes.

'Dr Audlin, I shall go mad if this goes on. I'm afraid to go to sleep. For two or three nights I haven't slept. I've sat up reading, and when I felt sleepy I put on my coat and walked until I couldn't walk any further. But I must have sleep. With all the work I have to do, my brain must be clear. I need rest; sleep brings me none. As soon as I fall asleep, my dreams begin, and he's always there, that common little devil, laughing at me. I don't deserve this treatment. I tell you, doctor, I'm not the man of my dreams; it's not fair to judge me by them. Ask anyone you like. I'm an honest, good man. No one can say anything against my moral character, either private or public. All I want is to serve my country. I have money, I have rank, so my life is easier than other men's. But I have always done my duty. I've given up everything to become the man I am. Greatness is my aim. Greatness is within my reach, and I'm losing my courage. I'm not that creature that Griffiths sees. I've told you three of my dreams: they're nothing; that man has seen me do things that are so shameful that I wouldn't tell them even if my life depended on it. And he remembers them. He has seen me do things that no man with any self-respect would do, things for which men are driven out of the society of others and sent to prison. He feels nothing but disgust for me and he no longer pretends to hide it. I tell you that if you can't do something to help me I shall either kill myself or kill him.'

'It's not a good idea to kill him,' said Dr Audlin calmly in his quiet voice. 'Your future would become even more uncertain.'

'I wouldn't be hanged for it, if that's what you mean. Who would know that I had killed him? That dream of mine has shown me how. I told you, the day after I'd hit him over the head with a bottle, he had a bad headache. He said so himself. That shows that he can feel with his waking body what happens to his body when he is asleep. I shan't hit him with a bottle next time. One night, when I'm dreaming, I shall find myself with a knife in my hand or a gun in my pocket. I must, because I want to so much. Then I shall seize my opportunity. I'll kill him; I'll shoot him like a dog. In the heart. And then I shall be free.'

Some people might have thought that Lord Mountdrago was mad. After all the years during which Dr Audlin had been treating the souls of men, he knew how thin the line is which divides those who are mad from those who are not. He knew that men who seemed healthy and appeared responsible citizens had such strange ideas in their minds, when you looked into them, that you could only call them mad. If you put them in a madhouse, not all the madhouses in the world would be large enough. But a man was not mad because he had strange dreams which had destroyed his courage. The case was unusual, but not unlike others which Dr Audlin had seen. He was doubtful, though, whether his methods of treatment would be of any use.

'Have you asked the advice of any other member of my profession?' he said.

'Only Sir Augustus. I simply told him that I suffered from very bad dreams. He said I was working too hard, and advised me to go away for a while. But I can't leave the Foreign Office just now, when the international situation needs all my attention. They can't do without me, and I know it. He gave me something to make me sleep. It had no effect.'

'Can you give me any reason why this particular man continues to feature in your dreams?'

'You asked me that question before. I answered it.'

That was true. But Dr Audlin had not been satisfied with the answer.

'Why should Owen Griffiths want to hurt you?'

'I don't know.'

Dr Audlin was sure that his patient was not speaking the truth.

'Have you ever harmed him?'

'Never.'

Dr Audlin saw before him a large, proud man who seemed to think that the questions put to him were insulting; but in spite of that he made you think of a frightened animal in a trap. Dr Audlin leaned forward and by the power of his eyes forced Lord Mountdrago to meet them.

'Are you quite sure?'

'Quite sure. He and I live different lives. I don't wish to say too much about it, but I must remind you that I am a Minister of the King and Griffiths is an ordinary member of the opposition party. Of course there's no social connection between us; he's a man from a much lower class, so he's not the sort of person I am likely to meet at any of the houses I go to. And politically we are far apart.'

'I can do nothing for you unless you tell me the complete truth.'

Lord Mountdrago's voice was cold. 'I am not used to having my word doubted, Dr Audlin. If you're going to do that, I think that to take up any more of your time can only be a waste of mine. If you will kindly tell my secretary what I owe you, he will send you a cheque.'

Dr Audlin's face showed no expression; you might have thought that he had not heard what Lord Mountdrago said. He continued to look steadily into his eyes, and his voice was serious and low.

'Have you done anything to this man that *he* might consider an injury?'

Lord Mountdrago paused. He looked away, and then looked back. He answered in a bad-tempered voice, 'Only if he was a dirty, low person.'

'But that is exactly what you've described him to be.'

Lord Mountdrago was beaten. Dr Audlin knew that he was at last going to say what he had until then held back. He dropped his eyes, and began drawing with his pencil. The silence lasted two or three minutes.

'If I didn't mention this before, it's only because it was so unimportant that I didn't see how it could be connected with the case. When Griffiths became a Member of Parliament, he began to make trouble almost immediately. His father's a miner, and he worked in a mine himself when he was a boy; he has also been a schoolmaster. He has the half-formed knowledge and useless dreams of a person of poor education. He's thin and grey-faced and never well dressed. His clothes are an insult to the House. His collar's never clean, and his tie's never tied properly. He looks as if he hasn't had a bath for a month, and his hands are dirty. But he is a good speaker, and he has some simple ideas on a number of subjects, and he is frequently asked to speak in the House. It appeared that he thought he knew something about foreign affairs, and some people listened to what he had to say. I heard stories that Griffiths might become Foreign Minister if another government came into power.

'One day I was speaking last in a discussion on foreign affairs. Griffiths had spoken before me for an hour. I thought it a good opportunity to destroy him, and by God, sir, I did. I tore his arguments to pieces. I showed the faults in his reasoning and his lack of knowledge. In the House of Commons the best way to attack someone is to make fun of him. I laughed at him, and the House laughed with me. Even some of Griffiths's friends could not help laughing at him. If ever a man was made to look a fool, I made Griffiths look a fool. I saw his face go white and soon he buried it in his hands. When I sat down I had killed him. I had destroyed his name for ever. He had no more chance of becoming Foreign Minister than the policeman at the door. I heard afterwards that his father, the old miner, and his mother had come to London with supporters from his home town to hear him speak.'

'So you ruined his political future?'

'Yes, I suppose so.'

'That is a very serious injury that you've done to him.'

'He brought it on himself.'

'Have you never felt at all sorry?'

'I think perhaps that if I had known his father and mother were listening, I would have been more gentle.'

There was nothing more for Dr Audlin to say, and he began to treat Lord Mountdrago in the manner that he thought best. He tried to make him forget his dreams when he awoke; he tried to make him sleep so deeply that he would not dream. But it was impossible. At the end of an hour he dismissed Lord Mountdrago. Since then he had seen him five or six times. He had done him no good. The terrible dreams continued every night. It was clear that his general condition was growing rapidly worse. He was very tired. He was very bad-tempered. He was angry because the treatment had not helped, but he continued it, because it seemed his only hope, and because he found it a help to talk openly. Dr Audlin felt that there was only one way in which Lord Mountdrago could be free from his troubles. After several visits the doctor managed to put him into a state of complete relaxation. Lord Mountdrago lay quite still, his eyes closed. Then Dr Audlin spoke the words which he had prepared.

'You will go to Owen Griffiths and say that you are sorry that you caused him that great injury. You will say that you will do whatever you can to undo the harm that you have done to him.'

The words acted on Lord Mountdrago like the blow of a whip across his face. He shook himself out of his sleep and jumped to his feet. His eyes burned and he poured out on Dr Audlin a stream of angry words such as even he had never heard. He swore at him. He shouted at him. He used such bad language that even Dr Audlin was surprised that he knew it.

'Say sorry to that dirty Welshman? I would rather kill myself.'

'I believe it to be the only way in which you can regain your calm.'

Dr Audlin had not often seen a man in such a state of uncontrolled anger. He grew red in the face and his eyes were sticking out of his head. Dr Audlin watched him calmly, waiting for the storm to end, and soon he saw that Lord Mountdrago, weakened by the troubles of so long a time, had no more strength.

'Sit down,' he said then, sharply.

Lord Mountdrago fell into a chair.

'I am tired,' he said; 'I must rest a minute and then I'll go.'

For five minutes perhaps they sat in complete silence. Lord Mountdrago was a proud man, but he was also a gentleman. When he broke the silence, he had regained his self-control.

'I'm afraid I've been very rude to you. I'm ashamed of the things I've said to you, and I'd understand if you refused to see me again. I hope you won't refuse. I think you're my only chance.'

'You mustn't worry about what you said. It's of no importance.'

'But there's one thing you mustn't ask me to do, and that is to say sorry to Griffiths.'

'I've thought a great deal about your case. I don't pretend to understand it, but I believe your only hope is to do what I suggest.'

'It's not my fault if I ruined him. I am not sorry.'

It was with these words that Lord Mountdrago had left the doctor.

◆

Dr Audlin read through his notes, and looked at the clock. It was six. It was strange that Lord Mountdrago had not come. His secretary had telephoned that morning to say that he would come at the usual hour. He must have been kept by important work. This idea gave Dr Audlin something else to think about: Lord Mountdrago was quite unfit to work and in no condition to deal with important matters of government. Dr Audlin wondered whether he ought to tell someone at the Foreign Office that it was dangerous to leave things to him just now.

But it would be difficult, and he would receive no thanks.

'After all,' he thought, 'politicians have caused so much trouble in the world during the last 25 years, I don't suppose it matters if they're mad or not.'

He rang the bell.

'If Lord Mountdrago comes now, will you tell him that I have another appointment at a quarter past six and so I'm afraid I can't see him.'

'Very good, sir.'

'Has the evening paper come yet?'

'I'll go and see.'

In a moment the servant brought it in. Across the top of the front page in big letters were the words: Death of a Foreign Minister.

'My God!' cried Dr Audlin.

For once he lost his usual calm. He was shocked, but he was not completely surprised. He had sometimes thought that Lord Mountdrago might kill himself, and he could not doubt that he had killed himself. The paper said that Lord Mountdrago had been waiting at an Underground station, and as the train came in he was seen to fall in front of it. It was supposed that he had suddenly fainted. The paper went on to say that Lord Mountdrago had been suffering for some weeks from the effects of overwork, but had felt it impossible to leave the Foreign Office. There was more about his love of his country, and about his skill, and various guesses about who would replace him as Foreign Minister. Dr Audlin read all this. He had not liked Lord Mountdrago. The chief feeling that his death caused in him was dissatisfaction that he had been able to do nothing to help him.

Dr Audlin felt discouraged, as he always did when he failed, and he was filled with disgust for the way in which he earned his living. He was dealing with dark forces that it was impossible for the human mind to understand.

He turned the pages of his paper in misery and hopelessness. But his misery turned once more to shock as his eyes fell on a paragraph near the bottom of a page. 'Sudden death of a Member of Parliament,' he read. 'Mr Owen Griffiths was taken ill in Fleet Street this afternoon, and when he was brought to the nearest hospital he was found to be dead. It is thought that death was from natural causes, but this is not certain.' Dr Audlin could hardly believe his eyes. Was it possible that, the night before. Lord Mountdrago had at last in his dream found a weapon, knife or gun, and had killed his enemy? And had that dream murder, in the same way as the blow from the bottle, taken effect a certain number of hours later on the waking man? Or was it, stranger and more frightening, that when Lord Mountdrago found a means of escape by killing himself, the enemy, still not satisfied, had followed him to some other world to continue his attacks there? It was strange. The sensible thing was to think of it as pure chance. Dr Audlin rang the bell.

'Tell Mrs Milton that I'm sorry I can't see her this evening. I'm not well.'

It was true; he was trembling. The dark night of the soul swallowed him up, and he felt a strange, deep fear of something that he did not understand.

ACTIVITIES

The Man Who Could Work Miracles

Before you read

1 Find these words in your dictionary. They are all in the story.

   astonish candle inn miracle roar

   a Which word is a place to stay?

   b Which word is a loud noise made by an animal?

   c Which word means the same as *surprise*?

   d Which word is something you can burn?

   e Do you believe in *miracles*? Describe a miracle you have read or heard about.

After you read

2 Describe:

   a Fotheringay's feelings about miracles at the start of the story.

   b the first miracle he performs.

   c the cause of Mr Winch's quarrel with him.

   d what Fotheringay believes Winch is doing in San Francisco.

   e the miracle Fotheringay works on Mrs Minchin.

   f the effects of his last miracle.

3 Continue the story. What do you think will happen next.

4 At what point does Fotheringay lose control of his new skill? What is his mistake, do you think?

The Model Millionaire

Before you read

5 The main character in this story is 'a charming, useless young man with perfect features and no profession' who needs ten thousand pounds before he can marry the girl he loves. List ways in which he might obtain this money.

6 Check the meanings of these words in your dictionary.

   Baron charm millionaire share shilling

Complete the puzzle using the new words.

Clue for word down

  1 title of an upper-class man

Clues for words across

  1 attractive quality which makes other people like you
  2 equal part into which the ownership of a company can be divided
  3 someone who has at least a million pounds or dollars
  4 unit of money

After you read

  7 Which of the people in the story ...
   a are in love?
   b has no money and no job?
   c is a painter?
   d is being painted?
   e is dresses as a beggar?
   f gives the beggar a pound?
   g helps Hughie to marry Laura?

  8 How do you react to beggars? Would you have done the same in Hughie's situation?

Lord Emsworth and the Girl Friend

Before you read

  9 Some upper-class British families live in very large houses in the country, surrounded by parks and areas of open land. What kind of relationship do you think they have with the people who work for them, and with those who live in the surrounding villages? How would the relationship have been different in the past?

100

10 Find these words in your dictionary. Use them to complete the sentences below.

fête   ladyship   misery   straw   top hat

  a My brother wore a .... to his friend's wedding.

  b The long cold winter caused great ..... to the people in the village.

  c It was a beautiful afternoon for the summer ....

  d Every day the farmer gave the horses fresh ....

  e The servants always addressed Lord Brown's wife as 'Your ......'

After you read

11 Who is speaking to whom, and about what?

  a 'Have you got your speech ready?'

  b 'Her ladyship likes the idea a lot.'

  c '… I threw a stone at 'im …'

  d '… if I knew him, I would shake him by the hand.'

  e 'Pretending to be a dog, sir, 'e was.'

  f 'This young lady would like some tea.'

  g 'These gardens … belong to me …'

12 Discuss the best adjectives to describe:

  a Lord Emsworth   **b** Lady Constance   **c** McAllister

  d Gladys   **e** Ern

The Doll's House

Before you read

13 Find the word *doll* in your dictionary. Did you have a doll's house when you were a child? Describe it or an imaginary one.

After you read

14 Explain:

  a why Isabel claims the right to tell other children about the doll's house.

  b why the lamp is so special to Kezia.

  c why the Kelvey children are avoided at school.

  d how Kezia feels about the Kelvey children.

  e how the Kelvey children feel when they are sent away from the doll's house.

15 Were/are there divisions between children from richer families and those from poorer families at your school? Compare the situation with the one described in the story.

X-ing a Paragraph

Before you read

16 What do you think the title of the story means?

17 Use your dictionary to check the meanings of these words:

article   edit

   a Which of the following might contain an *article*?

      (i) newspaper   (iv) a magazine

      (ii) a film   (v) a novel

      (iii) a song   (vi) a poem

   b An *editor*'s job is to *edit*. Where does an *editor* work?

      (i) in a factory   (iv) in a court

      (ii) in a shop   (v) in a film studio

      (iii) in a newspaper office

After you read

18 Fill the gaps to complete the story.

Bullet-head settles in Nopolis because ¹..... . In his first article, Bullet-head ²..... John Smith. In reply, John Smith suggests that Bullet-head uses the letter ³..... far too much. Bullet-head then writes an article in which almost every word ⁴..... . The printer's boy, though, uses the letter ⁵..... in place of ⁶..... because ⁷...... After this paragraph is printed, Bullet-head ⁸......

19 What do you think this story tells us about Poe's opinion of editors?

The Courtship of Susan Bell

Before you read

20 Find these words in your dictionary:

bless   courtship

   a Which one means to ask God to protect someone or something?

b *Courtship* is now an old-fashioned word. Why, do you think? In what ways has *courtship* in your country changed from the way it was in the past?

After you read

21 Answer the questions.

    a What effect does Mr Bell's death have on his family?

    b Why does Aaron Dunn first come to the house?

    c Why is Mrs Bell worried at first about allowing Dunn to stay?

    d How does Dunn try to show his love for Susan?

    e Why does Susan not receive the gift?

    f Why does Susan not give Dunn any sign of her own feelings?

    g What condition does Phineas Beckard put on their relationship?

    h Why does Susan become ill?

22 Take the parts of Aaron and Phineas. Act out the conversation in which Phineas tells Aaron to come back when he has a good job. Aaron's argument is that he already has one and should be allowed to marry Susan now.

23 Discuss the best adjective to describe the characters of:

    a Susan Bell   **b** Aaron Dunn   **c** Hetta Bell

24 Discuss why Hetta is against the relationship between Aaron Dunn and her sister.

Lord Mountdrago

Before you read

25 What do you dream about? Do your dreams ever affect you when you are awake? If so, how?

26 Find the meaning of *psychoanalyst* in your dictionary. A *psychoanalyst* specializes in examining a person's mind. What specialists in other parts of the human body can you name?

After you read

27 How are these things important in the story?

    a silk underclothes

    b "A Bicycle Made For Two"

    c a bottle

    d a miner

28 Explain how Dr Audlin believes that Mountdrago and Griffiths might have died.

29 Imagine you are Owen Griffiths. Explain how you felt after Mountdrago made you look a fool in the House of Commons in front of your parents.

Writing

30 Which story did you enjoy most? Explain why.

31 Choose a main character who changes dramatically in one of the stories. Describe how that person changes.

32 Choose one of the stories below. What does it tell us about the different social classes of the time?

   a 'Lord Emsworth and the Girl Friend'

   b 'The Doll's House'

   c 'Lord Mountdrago'

33 Write a newspaper article reporting Lord Mountdrago's death.

34 Two of the stories, 'Lord Emsworth and the Girl Friend' and 'X-ing a Paragraph' are humorous. Did you find them amusing. Give your reasons.

35 The letter Aaron Dunn wrote to Mrs Bell was very short. Write the love letter to Susan that he could have written instead, announcing that he was coming to ask her to marry him.